THE HERTFORD

A walker's gui

Edited by Bert Richardson

3rd Edition

Produced by The Friends of The Hertfordshire Way
Website www.fhw.org.uk
Email hertfordshireway@gmail.com

This book is dedicated to all those persons, known and unknown, who over the years have fought the good fight to protect and open up the footpath network in Hertfordshire. The paths that most of us take for granted would not be so freely accessible but for this band of dedicated walkers and campaigners who took on vested interests and won for us an excellent system of pathways.

There is still work to be done in our beloved Hertfordshire. This is a call to future generations to protect and seek to expand the network of footpaths so that they also leave behind a rich inheritance for future walkers to enjoy.

Walk not in vain
But with hope.
Hope that you will come again.
Or that others will walk this way
And share your joys.

First edition 1998
Second edition published June 2005
Reissued with amendments 2009
Reprinted November 2010
Third edition 2017
Publisher Reardon Publishing, PO Box 919, Cheltenham, GL50 9AN, England, www.Reardon.Biz

ISBN: 9781901037241

Contents

Acknowledgements

We would like to thank the following for financial help in funding this new edition and contributing to the purchase and erection of signs to show the route in a clockwise direction.

Major donors for the new guidebook edition and signs for the clockwise route

Bob Bemrose
Peter and Sue Garside
Graham Daniels
Alison and David Redcastle
Liz Deeble
The Robert Kiln Charitable Trust
North London and South Herts Ramblers
West Herts Ramblers
St Albans & District Footpath Society
Marion Wiseman
Ian and Val Hirst
Also to the many individual members who have contributed smaller amounts. Without those donations this guide book could not have been printed.

We would also wish to thank Celia Sanders for permitting us to use a selection of her watercolours from her diary “The Hertfordshire Way, A Journey” together with other photographers and artists for illustrations in this book. We also acknowledge all the leg wardens past and present who have contributed their time to this book both in writing and revising their part of the walk and for constantly monitoring the route.

Finally, a thank you to all who have enjoyed walking the route and who have sent their thanks and suggestions, some of which we have used in this Third Edition.

The following people have been involved in planning and revising the route since its creation in 1996.

David Allard, Michael Blackman, Anne Conchie, Allan Daniel, Graham Daniels, George & Joyce Faldo, Peter & Sue Garside, Mo Gilbert, Liz Hamilton, Bob Henbest, Eliza Hermann, Ian Hirst, David & Thelma Kealey, Hywel Morris, Ken Osborne, Chris Pagan, Bert Richardson, Michael & Nancy Scott, Carol & Harold Stokes, Peter Sutcliffe, Ron Tarling, John Telford, Angela Thomson, Roy Wheeler, Ian Whinnett, David Whiskin, Marion Wiseman, Dennis Zwolinski.

In Ashridge Estate (NT)

Preface to the Third Edition

In this guide there are a number of changes to the route from the previous edition which was published in 2009. We think they will give you further enjoyment of your walk. The changes are as follows:

Leg 12 There has been major changes to the whole of this leg so that we can avoid possible large housing development on the previous route into Bishop's Stortford.

Leg 13 The new bypass proposed for Little Hadham on the A120 would have meant a surface crossing of this bypass. The new route will allow us to cross it by a bridge and will take us further away from the noise of the traffic.

Leg 7 and 8 Route changes to these legs have been made to avoid some access concerns on leg 7 and on leg 8 safety improvements by avoiding a narrow and busy road.

Finally, we have made the guide more user friendly and refreshed the appearance with addition of a complete new set of photographs and sketches.

How the walk originated and has developed

In 1994 The Ramblers made plans to celebrate its sixty years fight to protect our national network of rights of way. Each area of the association was to plan its own celebration. The Hertfordshire and North Middlesex Area decided to do a long distance walk around the county. This was planned and organised by Bert Richardson who divided the route into 12 legs. Each volunteer leader walked their leg. In 1995, the Jubilee Year, over 60 people completed the walk. When the walk was completed a group remained interested in the route, and with the help of the local area of The Ramblers a committee was formed and the route was expanded to 166 miles in 14 legs. Twelve people started to survey the route and to write guides for each leg. Each leg was checked in the field by other volunteers and the whole work was brought together to form the first edition of this guide book. When you read it you will notice different styles of writing from each of the contributors. The background research in each leg was provided by the person(s) developing that section of the walk, with additional material by Bert Richardson. It was finally opened in 1998 after the guidebook was published and the waymarks were in position.

Hertfordshire Way Extension.

Since 2005 we have provided another way of going from Cuffley to Hertford as well as the original route. They are Leg 10A, from Cuffley to Broxbourne, incorporating a significant area of ancient woodland, and Leg 10B, from Broxbourne to Hertford, which takes in a large section of the Lee (or Lea) valley. Cuffley and Broxbourne are both accessible by train from Hertford (though from different stations in Hertford), so combining the two new legs with the original Leg 10 also offers a three-stage circular walk using public transport for access.

The Friends of The Hertfordshire Way

We are an independent organisation reliant on voluntary funding by members and friends sympathetic to our aims (see page 138).

Brief Background to The County of Hertfordshire

The 195 mile trail covers a large part of this beautiful, populous and rich county, incidentally one of the smallest counties in England, only 634 square miles. It is a county of rich contrasts. In the north-east there are wide open panoramas over low hills and farm lands as seen in the area around Barkway. Standing on Therfield Heath you can look down on to the flat plains of Cambridgeshire. Then in the south west there are the steep wooded escarpments of the Chilterns. The route visits ancient market towns, the Cathedral City of St Albans and countless picture postcard villages nestling in an intimate landscape of farmland and woods.

In 1801 Hertfordshire had a population of about 100,000; now it is well over one million. It has never been a heavily industrialised area but it has seen its own industrial changes from malting and brewing, plaiting of straw for hats, paper making, industries associated with wool such as fulling (cleaning the woven cloth) and silk mills. Today technical industries and service industries dominate the industrial scene.

A good introduction to the county, and how it developed from pre-history can be found in "The Hertfordshire Landscape" by Munby (1977) and "Hertfordshire, a Landscape History" by Rowe and Williamson (2013).

People have settled the area since prehistoric times. Along the very ancient Icknield Way there is evidence of many waves of people.

On Therfield Heath (see Leg 1) there is a long barrow of the Neolithic Age (2500 BC) and round barrows of the Bronze Age (1000 BC). There is evidence of the Beaker People in Hertfordshire. The hill forts of the Iron Age settlers gave way at the height of their power to the might of the Roman invasion. Many Roman roads go through Hertfordshire, e.g. Ermine Street and Watling Street, and our walk crosses the remains of the Roman town of Verulamium (St Albans).

In the Dark Ages Hertfordshire was part of the shifting boundary between the English settlers (Angles & Saxons) and the later invaders, the Vikings. It was a long and turbulent time before the country became united. A good novel, which covers this period, is the "Conscience of the King" by Alfred Duggan.

In the Medieval period the great abbeys were founded and one can still be seen in St Albans (see Legs 4 & 5). Many fine Medieval churches can be seen on this walk and short detours will be worth your while to seek out some of these (unfortunately due to the presence of valuable historic items most country churches are now locked on weekdays).

During the 16th to 18th centuries many country estates were established in Hertfordshire e.g. Hatfield House, Knebworth House and Ashridge House. Some of the houses have not survived but our walk will take you through parkland, which reminds the walker of those estates. Walkers passing through Ayot St Lawrence will be going through such parkland and Ashridge still has its great house. It was first a monastery, then a great house, now a management college.

The growth of London and the coming of industry saw some rapid development in the county in the 19th and 20th centuries. An example of this development was the Ovaltine factory at Kings Langley with the model farm to feed its need for eggs and milk. The factory and farms are all now sadly gone (see Legs 7 & 8).

No major rivers flow through the county, however it is still famous for the large number of chalk streams and their associated wildlife (the River Lee or Lea, a tributary of the Thames has its source just north of Luton, flows though the county and is navigable up to Hertford). The Grand Union Canal passes through our county on its way north west (see Leg 7). The railways opened up Hertfordshire for industry and settlement and such towns as Hemel Hempstead and Watford grew from several hundred people to 80,000 plus. Many of the great road routes, which fan out from London (such as the A1, A5, A6, A10 and M1) pass through our county. Finally we saw the first garden cities (Letchworth and Welwyn Garden City) and the new town of Stevenage.

The great orbital road, the M25, cuts its way through the county (see Legs 7 to 9) not forgetting the electricity pylons, supplying our thirst for power.

Many famous people are associated with Hertfordshire. Samuel Pepys was a regular visitor who once when staying in Baldock noticed that the landlady was very pretty but “I durst not take notice of her, her husband being there”. Queen Elizabeth I, then a princess, was a virtual prisoner at Hatfield House when the Roman Catholic Queen Mary was on the throne. King James I had a palace at Royston (the start of our walk) from where he hunted on the lands of north Hertfordshire.
The so called Rye House Plot to kill King Charles II was hatched on its borders. Izaac Walton of “Compleat Angler” fame knew the River Lea well. The earliest Christian martyr, St Alban, was executed in Roman times at the site of the city bearing his name. Francis Bacon lived at Gorhambury (an estate near St Albans through which our walk passes). He is buried in the church of St Michael nearby. George Bernard Shaw made his home in Ayot St Lawrence; his home is now a National Trust property and is close to our route. George Orwell, Barbara Cartland, Charles Lamb and W. E. Johns lived in the county.

In spite of the development, most of your walking will be on rural pathways through fields, villages and woods where you can enjoy the peace and forget the might and noise of industry that remind you of the century we live in —— Good walking

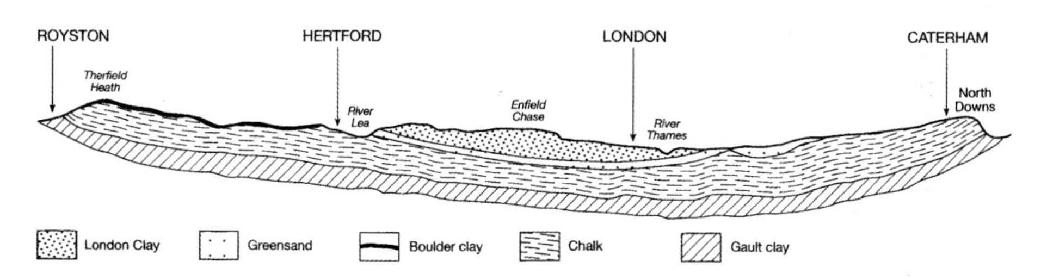

Royston is built at the base of the chalk hills. This scarp slope of chalk slowly dips under the London Basin to re-appear as the North Downs, south of London. On the top of the scarp the chalk is covered with boulder clay (which is why the footpaths in the country are sometimes sticky in winter) deposited in the last Ice Age.

Walking The Hertfordshire Way

General notes for the walker

In the guidebook the walk is described in an anticlockwise direction and it is waymarked in both directions (see the two distinctive roundels).

Sign posts at most road crossings mark the route in the anticlockwise direction.

The walk is conveniently divided into 16 legs which are between 9 and 15 miles in length. In addition to the written text each leg has a map of the route. The description for each leg has been written so that it is possible to follow the route without recourse to a map though we do recommend the use of Ordnance Survey Explorer Maps to give additional enjoyment to your walk. Also included in the text are notes of places of interest that you pass or can deviate to view.

The walk has been divided into legs for two reasons. Each leg gives a good day's walking for the average walker. We have fitted the beginnings and ends of the legs into public transport, as near as is possible in these days of restricted public transport. This does not restrict the walker into a straitjacket. Individual walkers can plan their own approach to the walk. Because each leg is divided into numbered sections individuals can plan their own starting and finishing points and stop at a chosen mileage suitable to their inclinations. This walk is not a route march. We want the walker to savour and enjoy one of the finest waymarked long distance routes in England.

On this walk there are many fine villages, historic towns and other interesting tourist sites. For example, the remains of the Roman city (Verulamium) at St Albans and the beautiful Ashridge Estate (NT). There is also a fine selection of public houses for lunch time refreshment. Almost all the walk is on public rights of way (there are a few sections on permissive paths but they are clearly noted in the text). Hertfordshire is one of the more enlightened counties concerning public rights of way and most are clearly marked. The main problem is the non-reinstatement of cross field paths after ploughing or cropping or allowing crops to grow on them.

The second major problem is the ploughing up of paths on the edges of fields. Both these practices are illegal and should be reported. If you find these problems, or any other, on your walk please write to Hertfordshire County Council, Environmental Management Department, Rights of Way, County Hall, Hertford. SG13 8DN. State the date of your observations, what the problem is, and the place and grid reference, if possible.

Please note public rights of way are the Queen's Highway and you have a legal right to be on them at any time. They have a legal status. It is important to remember that over the years many people have campaigned to keep these paths open for the public to enjoy. The main protector of these rights is The Ramblers. Membership of this group is recommended as it provides three walking magazines a year full of useful and important information including pages of bed and breakfast accommodation in Britain. You can also become a member of a local walking group.

The address is: The Rambler, 2nd Floor, Camelford House, 87-90 Albert Embankment, London SE1 7 TW

Respect for the countryside

Hertfordshire is a farming county so please close and fasten all gates which you have opened. Dogs must be kept on leads among stock and close to woodland where game birds could be nesting. When not on a lead they should be at heel at all times and not rushing about the countryside frightening the wild life and other walkers. Please do not leave any rubbish; take it home with you.

Safety
Safety is important at all times around farm machinery and industrial sites but two areas of safety are very important: roads and railway lines. Even the narrow roads, which we will cross and walk along at times, can carry fast-moving traffic, so be vigilant and obey the rules of safety. If you are walking in a party make sure the whole group is made aware of your approach to roads. Occasionally it is necessary to cross main line railways; do this with extreme care.

Clothing
This is lowland Britain and the most important item is footwear. Strong supportive footwear and thick socks are recommended. Hertfordshire is a county of clay and it can be very muddy in winter. Always carry waterproofs in Britain! It is also recommended that you carry a basic first aid kit.

The route
The route is meant to be followed by reading the detailed text. The maps included in each leg are for information as to direction and places and not for detailed route guidance. They will be useful for reference to Ordnance Survey maps.

Additional information in the text
In addition to the maps and the detailed walking text there is background information which is provided for those not familiar with the area and which we hope will increase your enjoyment as you travel through this beautiful county.

Maps
We recommend that you do the walk with the Ordnance Survey Explorer Map as your companion as this is the best scale for route finding. Landranger maps cover a larger area than the above map and are good for general directions but are more difficult to follow when walking, as their scale is smaller.

Public transport, refreshments and parking on route
Each leg has reference to public transport availability. The text also refers to places where refreshments can be obtained but do be aware that pubs and shops sometimes close with very little notice. We have

tried to list car parking as three types: free, pay and street parking. It's up to you to search them out!
Cars: If you are using your car please park with due consideration for landowners and residents in the area. Do remember on Sundays not to use church parking spaces.

When using the guide book please note
Great care has been taken to ensure that the descriptions of the route are as accurate as possible but various factors affect the final printed word and individual interpretations of the written word do vary! Also features on the land can change, for example houses can be built or repainted and new hedges planted. Stiles and gates can rot and may not be replaced immediately; they can be replaced by kissing gates (Hertfordshire County Council policy).

Walkers near Clothall

Travel and Tourism

In previous editions of the guidebook we included a chapter on tourist information centres and public transport in the County. Much has changed in the last 20 years; the internet has made many printed sources redundant and we recommend that you seek up-to-date information online. At the date of publication of this guidebook there are tourist information centres in.

Baldock (01438 737 333)

Bishop's Stortford (01279 715 001)

Harpenden (01582 768 278)

Hertford (01992 584 322)

Letchworth (01462 487 868)

St Albans (01727 864 511)

Stevenage (0300 123 4049)

Tring (01442 823 347)

Ware (01920 487 848)

Overnight accommodation (hotels, pubs and B&B) is available in all the main towns and some villages but we have not attempted to provide a list here.

There is some information about car-parking and public transport in the introduction to each leg of the walk. This was valid at the time of publication of this guidebook but you will be aware that availability of both car-parks and public transport can change as local authorities revise their budgets. What follows is some more general advice about transport.

Firstly, spend some time on planning. If you have two cars you will be familiar with the process of leaving one car at the end-point of the walk and driving in the other car to the start. With just one car you can – for most legs – complete the return journey to your parked car by public transport. Experience has shown that on several of the legs, travelling one way by bus or train has been at least as quick as using two cars with the need to shuttle between start and finish points, not to mention the need to find (and pay for) parking, so even for those who don't yet have the benefit of free bus travel, there is some sense in considering public transport as an alternative to car.

Several people have done the entire route of nearly 200 miles using only public transport to get to the start of each leg and to return home at the end. The experiences of those who have done so lead to some general principles (since everyone will have a different starting point it's not practical to give a stage-by-stage account from various places). There are three legs (**7** Tring to Kings Langley; **10** Cuffley to Hertford and **10B** Broxbourne to Hertford) where train is the quickest way – if not the cheapest - of getting between the end point and the start; all you have to consider is how to get to one end or the other of these legs. If you have the choice, it's better to do the return journey by train so as to avoid the early morning rush hours with the associated cost (you can't normally get discounted fares for early morning journeys). In addition, it's worth bearing in mind that 8 of the 15 'nodes' on the Hertfordshire Way are at, or close to, railway stations: Royston (legs 1 and 14), St Albans (legs 4 and 5), Tring (legs 6 and 7), Kings Langley (legs 7 and 8), Cuffley (legs 9, 10 and 10A), Broxbourne (legs 10A and 10B), Hertford (legs 10, 10B and 11), and Bishop's Stortford (legs 12 and 13). So if you live close to a station on the relevant railway line, or can easily get there by bus, you should consider using the train for that leg. One 'node' (Wallington) is a problem as it no longer has a bus service, but it isn't far to the edge of Baldock where there are buses and trains. Nevertheless, most people will have to use buses for the great majority of the time. The first thing, if you don't already know them by heart, is to study the timetables for any bus routes that pass close to your house. Having done that, work out how best to get to one or more of the major bus interchanges in the county: Watford, St Albans, Stevenage, WGC, Hertford, Bishop's Stortford. From there you will have access to the main bus network which feeds into the minor routes.

The Traveline South East website is very useful, but needs careful interpretation. The journey planner is a good place to start, but does not always give the best answer. It asks you to enter a starting point and a finishing point for your journey, and to specify a date and time for travel; there are other parameters you can enter to refine the search, but those are the essentials. The system then offers you a selection of routes and methods for completing your journey (including train and tube, if appropriate). Not all of these will be sensible; remember that they are worked out by the computer using a 'logical' algorithm, not by a real person who understands what you want to do. One point to note is that the computer likes to send you *via* London mainline terminals and the underground (even when there are quicker and shorter routes) unless you tell it not to. When you have found out which bus services are involved, go to the Traveline South East timetable option and study the actual timetables and the bus route maps. It is sometimes possible to improve on the journey planner by choosing a different bus number from the one recommended, or changing buses at a different place. However, if your journey involves a change of buses, the journey planner tends to give you a reasonable leeway to allow for delays; choosing your own route might not!

If you choose to travel by public transport we recommend that you always have a 'Plan B' when you set out. Buses can be delayed or early or even cancelled altogether; in case you miss a vital connection you should always be prepared with an alternative. On occasion a 'Plan C' may be advisable: that is, the phone number of a local taxi operator in case you get stranded in a remote location where the buses are very infrequent.

Open fields leading to Ash Valley

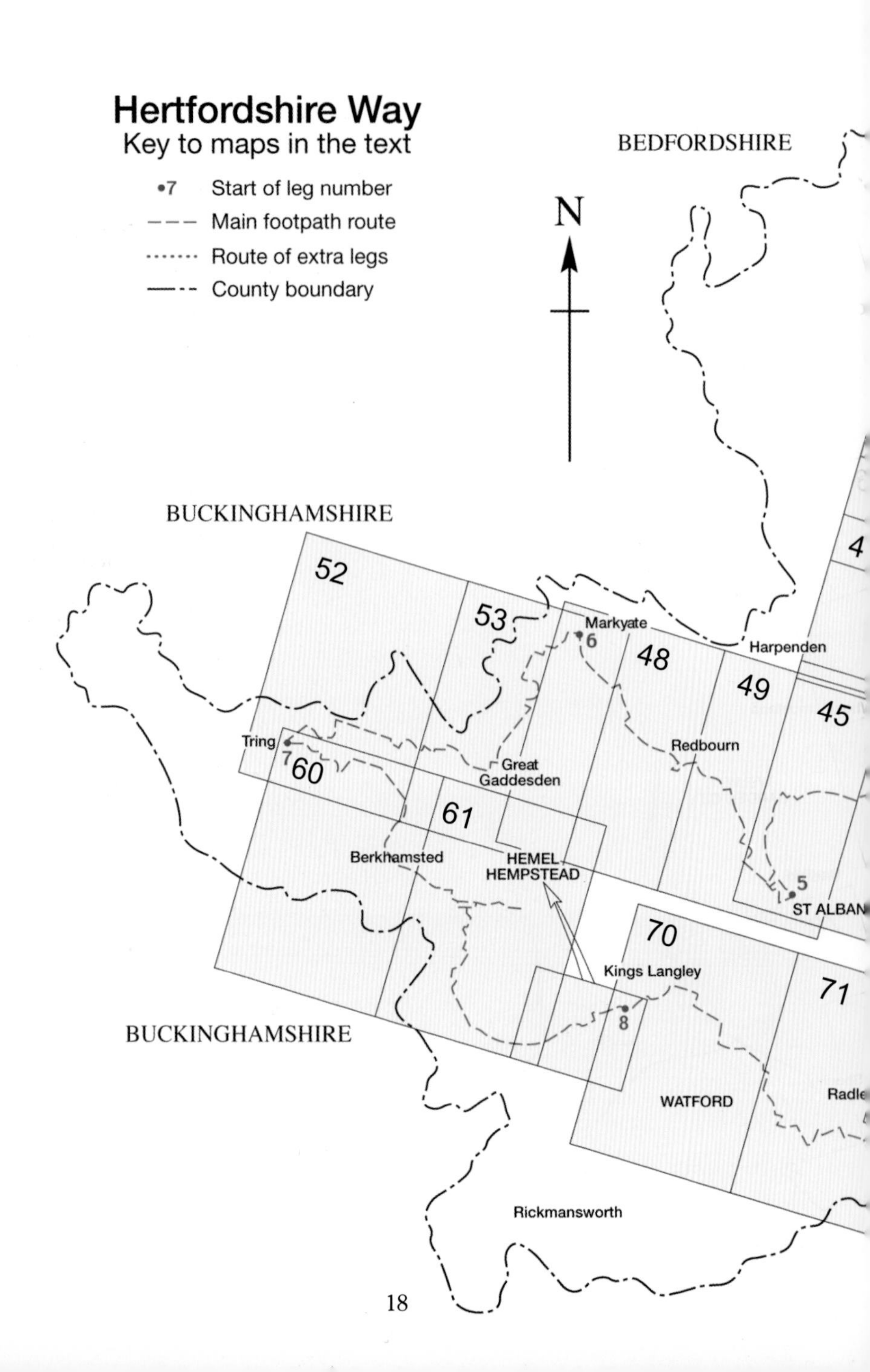
Hertfordshire Way
Key to maps in the text
•7 Start of leg number
Main footpath route
Route of extra legs
County boundary
BEDFORDSHIRE
N
BUCKINGHAMSHIRE
52
53
Markyate
6
48
Harpenden
49
45
Tring
7
60
Great
Gaddesden
Redbourn
61
Berkhamsted
HEMEL
HEMPSTEAD
5
ST ALBAN
70
Kings Langley
71
8
BUCKINGHAMSHIRE
WATFORD
Radle
Rickmansworth

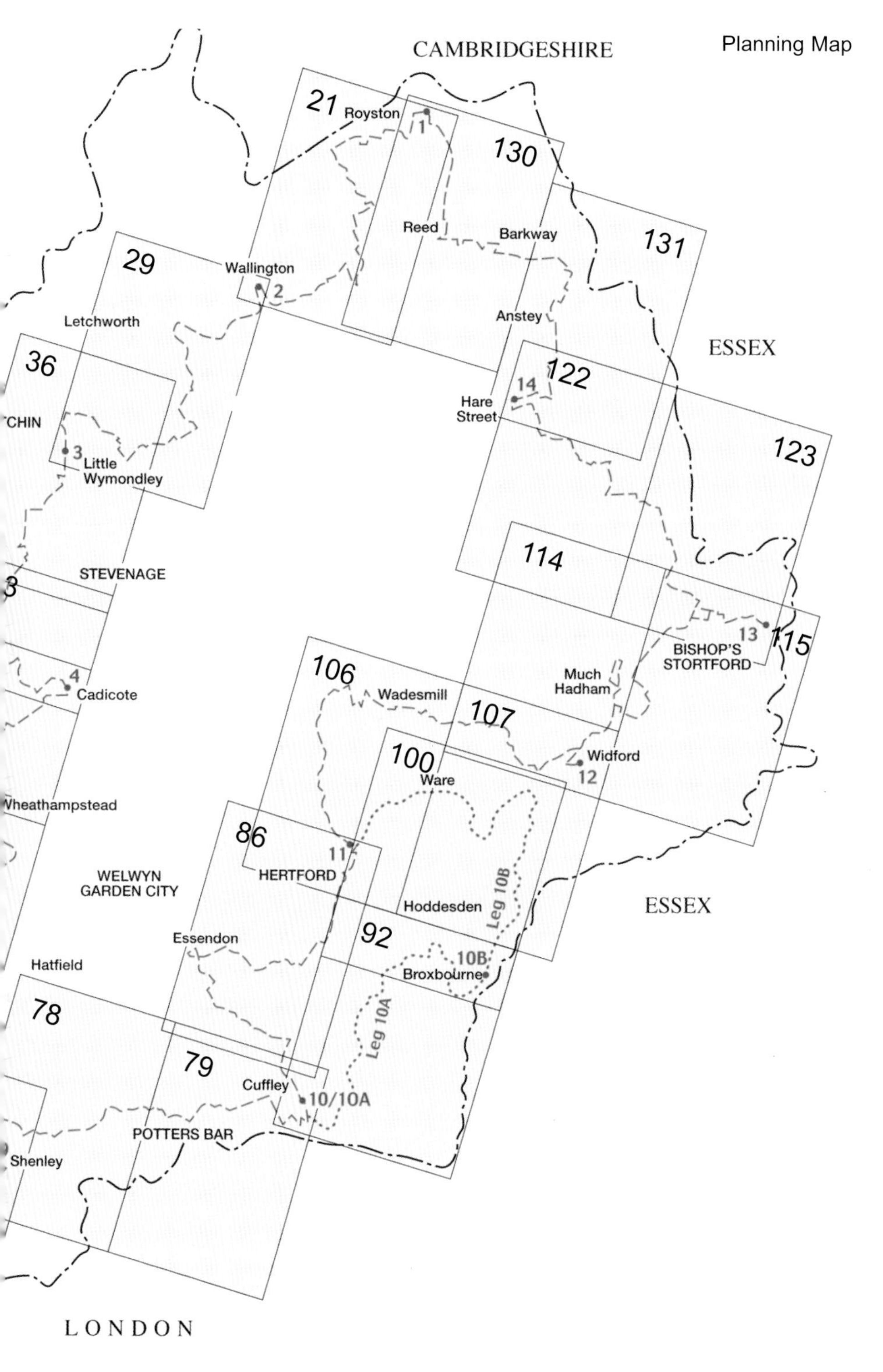
CAMBRIDGESHIRE
21
Royston
1
130
Reed
Barkway
131
29
Wallington
2
Letchworth
Anstey
ESSEX
36
122
14
Hare
Street
CHIN
123
3
Little
Wymondley
114
STEVENAGE
13
115
BISHOP'S
STORTFORD
106
Much
Hadham
4
Cadicote
Wadesmill
107
100
Widford
12
Ware
Wheathampstead
86
11
HERTFORD
Leg 10B
WELWYN
GARDEN CITY
Hoddesden
ESSEX
92
Essendon
10B
Broxbourne
Hatfield
Leg 10A
78
79
Cuffley
10/10A
POTTERS BAR
Shenley
LONDON

Leg 1 Royston to Wallington

Length 11.1 miles.
Start The Cross, Royston SG8 5AY, TL 356407. Pay parking in the town, free on the heath 0.5 miles west along Baldock Road, SG8 5BG, TL 347404.
Finish Wallington in small free car park, SG7 6SW, TL 293338. Extra parking available in lay by on road to Baldock.
Maps Explorer 209, 192, 193, Landranger 153, 154, 166.
Public Transport Royston has regular bus and train services to major centres. Wallington has no service to speak of but is only 3.5 miles from Baldock, which has trains and buses.
Pubs/Refreshments The only pub is in Therfield, 5 miles into the walk.

The Route

This is the most dramatic leg from the scenery point of view, with the first half of the walk climbing and following the scarp slopes of the chalk hills. Once on the top we come into a gentle rural landscape of fields and hedgerows with gently rolling hills, so typical of Hertfordshire. On the heath there is a long barrow and several round barrows (see introduction).
We are starting in the north of the county in Royston, a busy, small market town. It has a range of industries including Johnson Matthey, who include gold refining among their many skills. Historically it grew up where an old Roman road crosses the prehistoric Icknield Way. It was not a Saxon parish but grew around a Priory established by the Normans. The Icknield Way long distance path passes through the town and crosses our route in several places. Royston has a market on Wednesday and Saturday, a library, a museum and an ample supply of public houses. It has a unique cave, cut into the chalk in medieval times, with interesting carvings in the chalk.The Parish Church is part of the old priory with a Victorian chancel, and is worth a visit. Royston was the centre from where King James I hunted on the open chalk downlands. There is very little of his palace remaining. Therfield Heath on the edge of the town is a small remnant (2 miles long by ½ mile deep) of that vast hunting ground. A very good guide to the town can be obtained from the library. If you are staying in Royston there are lots of places to visit in the area.

The Walk

1. We start the walk in the centre of the town at the Cross located on the south side of Baldock Street at the junction with Kneesworth Street. (Notice the large stone, Royse Stone, which was the base of the medieval cross). Turn west along Baldock Street and walk out of the town in a westerly direction. Cross Princes Mews then Briary Lane with your road climbing gently to the heath. The footway ends just before Therfield Heath which starts where you reach the golf club house and you turn left onto the heath. You can go behind or in front of the golf club house. Your aim is to follow the path along the heath's eastern and southern boundary to the top of the valley. After the club house follow the footpath keeping a hedge and fences on your left which will end leaving an open field. Continue climbing steadily until you regain a hedge on your left, climbing round a clump of trees on your left before descending slightly.

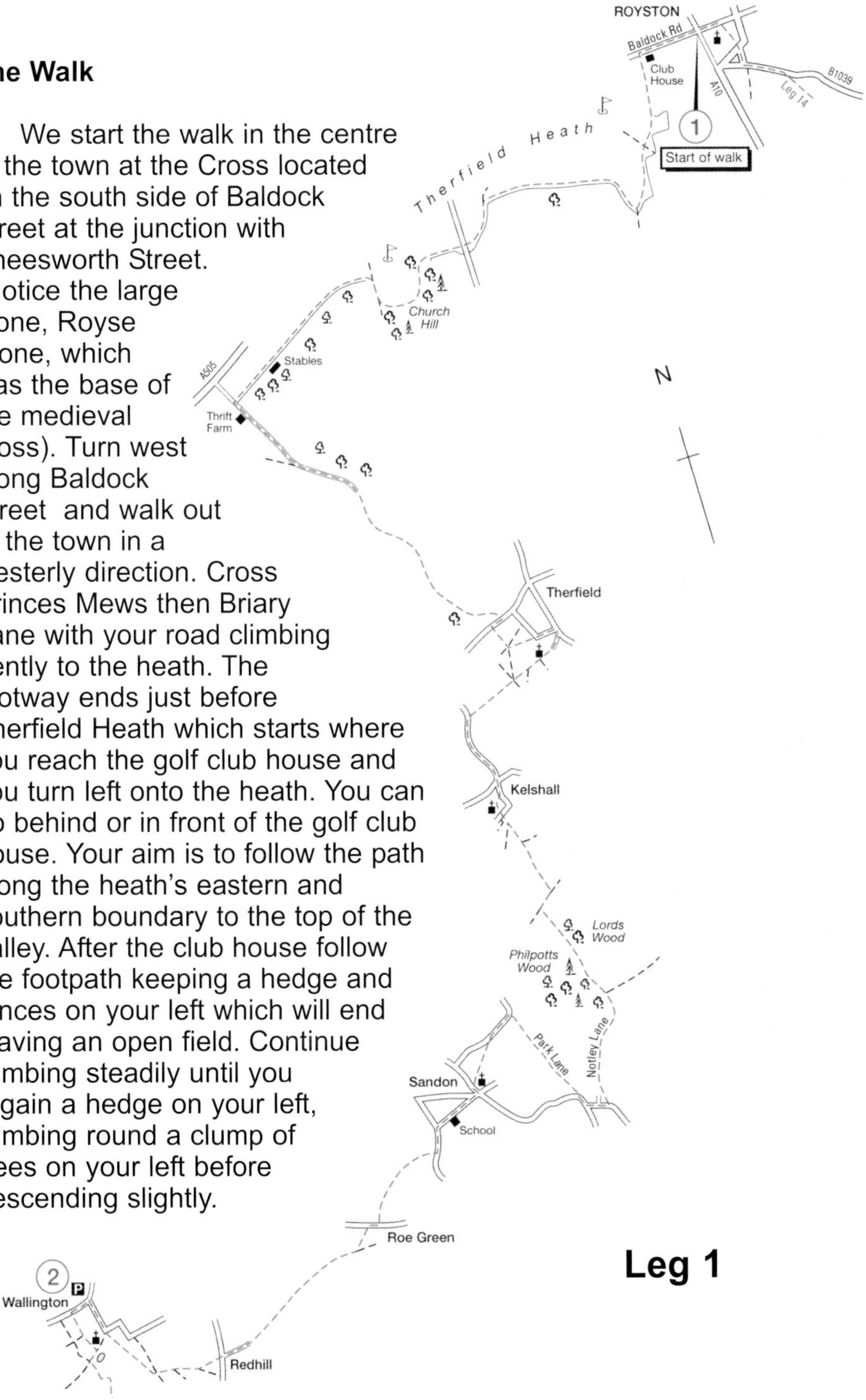

After a short descent continue to follow the path which moves towards the centre of the valley and starts to climb again. At a crossroads of footpaths turn left up a small gulley leading to the top of the valley where you will find an information board and ramblers gate.
Do not pass through the ramblers gate but almost turn back on yourself and follow the path on your left downhill entering the trees. Continue downhill on this path keeping view of the open field on your left, up some steps until coming out again to open heath land with the golf course on your right.
This golf course is on common land and you have a right to explore the heath and its several barrows but do take care crossing any golf fairways.
Follow the footpath keeping to the southern edge of the heath, going in and out of the trees, until you come to a gravel path. Turn left on this path as you go round another steep valley. Enter a small wood on a clear path, taking the right hand fork in the middle of the wood which brings you out to the Therfield road (1.9 miles).

2. Cross the road diagonally left, through a ramblers gate up some steps into trees, following a clear track. After about 300 yards look out for the entrance on your left to Jubilee Wood together with The Jubilee Stone, an engraved boulder, 4 ft high (it can be hidden by vegetation in summer). Continue on this track past another information board into some large beech trees (Fox Covert Nature reserve). Follow the wide track, which gradually turns to the left (south) continually looking right for another information board close to the edge of the trees.
Turn right past the information board and onto Church Hill. The steep drop to your left will have a flat, wide dry valley bottom if you are on the correct hill! Walk along its crest, at first descending slowly and then steeply to your right to a ramblers gate.
While on the top stop to admire the magnificent views all around you especially to the north and west over the flat Cambridgeshire landscape. If you are here in spring you may be lucky enough to see the Pasque flowers on this hill (do not pick or uproot them) and July/early August the rare Chalk Hill Blue butterfly.
Go through the ramblers gate and turn right along a track until you come to the golf course. On reaching the golf course turn left with a tall thick beech hedge on your left and open heath on your right. Be careful here that you have not gone on to a track into a field with a hedge on both sides! You should have the open heath on your right with the A505 below you. You follow this hedge, which soon becomes a tree hedge, keeping it on your immediate left until reaching the western end of the Heath and Thrift Farm (3.3 miles).

Church Hill with Pasque flower and Chalk Hill Blue

3. Turn left through the wooden gate into the farmyard and walk between the buildings. Go straight on along the farm track (south east) initially with a hedge on your left and then a square mesh fence on your left. At the end of the mesh fence follow the track between open fields through a gap with a hedge on your left and the rifle range (built on the site of an old farm) on your right.
This is an active range so do not be alarmed if you hear gunfire whilst walking this stretch.
Continue following the hedge as it gradually thins out until you reach a guide post. Here you leave the hedge and go slightly right, crossing between open fields towards a hedge and trees where you will find another guide post. Keep this hedge to your right and soon enter a gully deep in trees (it can be wet and very slippery here in winter). You climb this gully and go through a kissing gate to a road on the edge of Therfield (4.8 miles).

4. Turn right, going past on your left a group of houses built from a converted farm building and finally the converted farmhouse. At the end of its garden take the footpath on your left. Look out for some iron gates on your right, opposite them is the first of two drives where you will get your first glance of Tuthill Manor.

Tuthill Manor

This beautiful old manor house was a cowshed until it was discovered in the 1970s and fully restored to its former glory. You will see more of it in a moment.

On reaching a water tower on your right look out for two footpaths in the hedge on your left. Taking the second footpath on your left cross over a stile to enter the field heading straight for the centre with Tuthill Manor on your left. Now strike out diagonally right across the field on an indistinct path among the mounds of an ancient motte and bailey castle. Look out for a stile in the hedge on your left. Cross the stile to enter the garden of a large house (the house can be seen on the right with the church tower behind it); go straight ahead through a gap, pass a pond on your left keeping tight to the hedge on your left down the drive to the road where you turn right to Therfield Green.

You pass some fine old houses. Just before the village green notice the fine half-timbered house on your right (Forge House), which was the village smithy. The road divides around a village green (5.2 miles). *Opposite you at the other side of the village green is the Fox and Duck pub and restaurant. To the left of the pub is the site of the original village school; notice the original school plaque (dated 1855) in front of the houses.*

5. On reaching the green turn immediately right into the cul de sac, Church Lane, (opposite the pub) to the church and enter the church grounds at the end of the road. Take the footpath round the left of the church and out through the gate in front of the church porch. When you exit the churchyard gate turn right on to the track. After about a hundred yards a track joins from the right; we go straight on. Continue straight on passing over a wooden bridge, through a kissing gate, until you meet a road on the edge of Kelshall. Turn left on to this road and walk through the pretty village passing a pond on your right, a studio and pottery on your left. Pass the village hall, ignoring the road on your left bear right to Kelshall Street.
Notice in the middle of this road the village green and its new Millennium obelisk. It must be the smallest village green in England.
Soon the road turns right but go straight on into the cul de sac to the church. After 80 yards look for a footpath on your right and follow this into a churchyard (6.1 miles).
In the churchyard is a much damaged base of a fifteenth century cross.
Follow the path round the left side of the church and out through the main gate but take time to explore the church. Cross the road and go through the five bar gate opposite looking for a kissing gate in the wooden fence on your right. Go through it and follow the path between fences and through two more kissing gates in quick succession. Keeping your direction, cross another a field and through a fourth kissing gate, then on through a narrow field through a fifth kissing gate out into open fields aiming for a white marker post. At the white marker post take the footpath slightly diagonally right to another white marker post on the opposite side of this large field. On reaching the second marker post drop down steps to a wide farm track making a T junction to your path (6.6 miles).

6. Turn right onto this track and follow it for about 200 yards and take the next track on your left. You will initially pass between open fields, then pass Lords Wood on your left and then pass Philpotts Wood on your right. The path bears left round the edge of the wood and soon reaches a wide gap in the trees. Turn right through this wide gap in the hedge over a stream and ignoring a gate on your right, the footpath on your left proceeds straight ahead to follow a sunken hedge-lined bridleway until you reach a drive to a house, turn left here and reach the public road. Turn right to a road junction, right again and when the road turns sharply left take a bridleway on your right (7.7 miles).

7. Follow this bridleway with trees on both sides. You will come out on a sharp corner onto a road. Turn left onto this road keeping an eye out for a footpath (150 yards) on your left. Take this path and you will come out in the back of Sandon Churchyard (8.3 miles). The church is worth a visit.

Sandon Pond

8. Take the footpath round the right side of the church coming out of the churchyard by the lych gate, turn left on to the road, which almost immediately takes you to a T junction. Go right with the village green on your right and pond on your left. Soon you will pass a school on your left, then follow the road when it turns sharp left. Now look out for the next footpath on your right. Two paths leave the road at this point; pass through the kissing gate and take the right hand one diagonally left across the meadow to two kissing gates in the fence. Pass through these kissing gates and keeping your diagonal direction pass through two more kissing gates with a wooden bridge in between. Follow the track slightly left through a field to a further two kissing gates with a

track in between. Continue directly ahead to another kissing gate, pass through this gate and follow the path round to the left between fences reaching another kissing gate. Pass through this kissing gate following the path to another kissing gate over a small bridge and through trees out to the road. You will emerge on to a wide green with a road running through the middle. Cross the road to a gravel drive. Walk up the drive and look out for a narrow footpath on your right taking you between houses to a field. Pass through a kissing gate, cross the field to the far right hand corner through another kissing gate, and over a bridge to a track. Turn right and follow this track for about a mile to a road at Redhill (10.3 miles).

9. Cross the road to another footpath follow this footpath slightly diagonally left across a field to a wooden bridge, which crosses a shallow ditch. Cross the ditch and climb steadily (slightly right) to a hedge and keep climbing with the hedge on the right. Reaching a junction of paths at an opening between trees go diagonally right taking the second footpath on the right diagonally right across a field aiming for a kissing gate just to the right of the farm silos. Pass through the kissing gate and across the meadow, which leads down to Wallington. Pass through a final kissing gate to the road directly in front of you turning right pass the pond on your left into the village. Do not take the Sandon Road. Soon you will be in the centre of the village. You have finished Leg 1 when you come to a sharp left turn in the road (11.1 miles). Turn right here to a small car park on your left.

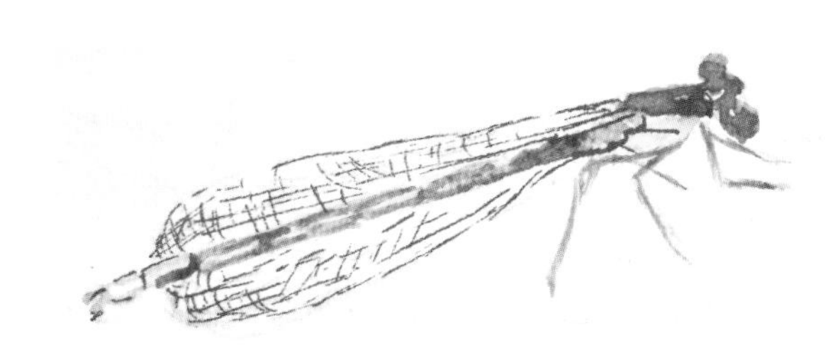

Leg 2 Wallington to Little Wymondley

Length 12.2 miles.
Start Wallington in small free car park, SG7 6SW, TL 293338.
Finish Little Wymondley, SG4 7HY, TL 215274.
Maps Explorer 193, Landranger 166.
Public Transport Wallington (see Leg 1). Little Wymondley has an hourly bus service, Luton & Hitchin to/from Stevenage.
Pubs/Refreshments Weston (two pubs) Graveley (two pubs) Great Wymondley (one pub) and Little Wymondley (two pubs).

The Route

Planes,Trains and Automobiles. An almost entirely rural leg, all the more surprising for it passes close to the new town of Stevenage, crosses the A1(M), and catches sight of planes coming into Luton. The East Coast Main Line is crossed at the end of the Leg.

The Walk

NB The right of way off Kits Lane in Wallington is under review. We describe the most likely route but look for signs for a left turn along Kits Lane

1. There is a small car park in The Street in Wallington. From the car park turn back up The Street, right into Kits Lane and continue on for a further 100 yards.
On the corner of Kits Lane notice a plaque on a cottage on your right to commemorate George Orwell who lived here for a period.

Then take the footpath up steps on your left, which leads to the church. (If part of the footpath is overgrown, divert along the side of the meadow). Go out through the gate (pond opposite) turn right onto a metalled track and follow it as it turns left. It becomes a farm track and turns left then right.

2. After about 400 yards look out for a waymark to your left and almost immediately following there will be a further waymark to your right, off the main track; take this footpath. Keep a hedge on your right. After 800 yards you will cross a footbridge to enter a wood; it is well waymarked so you should have no difficulty with your route. On coming out of the wood keep the next wood on your left. Baldock is two miles away, on your right hand side, and you may catch a glimpse of it. Soon you will walk between two hedges.

3. When you reach a busy road, A507, do not use the footpath continuing on the other side. Wherever you cross remember it is an A road with fast traffic. The route uses a footpath 50 yards to your right along this road. There a footpath leaves the other side. However, it is possible to cross the road at the point where you arrived and a well used track goes half right and connects to the right of way after 100 yards saving the roadside walk.

Whether you use the right of way or the well-used track, the route across the field to the village is not waymarked after the road. The field is usually only partly cultivated and a route is usually visible heading generally west, diverging from the road at about 45 degrees.

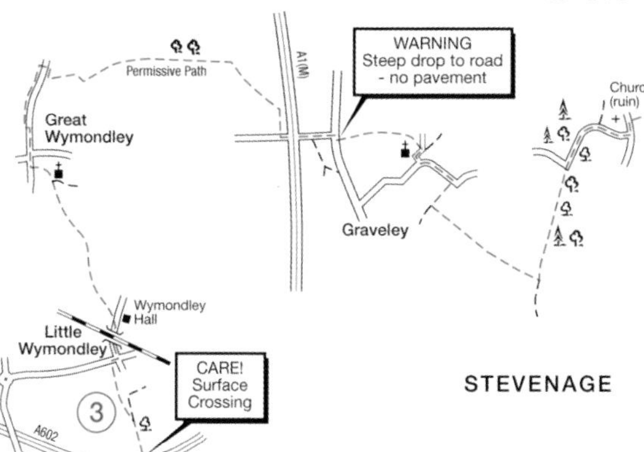

If you miss it, go round the edge of the field anticlockwise and you will reach the right place.
After 500 yards, approaching a house, go down some steps to the road and turn left. Clothall Church is on your right but is hidden in summer (2.3 miles).

The church is well worth a visit. It has some fine monumental brasses, one commemorating John Ventner, Rector in 1404 and another to the wife and sixteen children of William Bramfield.

4. When the road suddenly turns left you turn right down a bridleway leading to a path across the centre of a field. Baldock Church is now almost straight ahead of you.

5. The A507 can be seen and heard on your right. Follow this route crossing other paths and keep heading for the farm buildings ahead. When you reach the farm buildings turn left between them and into a field with a hedge on your right. At the end of the field go through the gate and turn sharp left. The field edge path becomes a track and climbs steeply. Continue on this track, ignoring side tracks. The track becomes level and half a mile after a right hand bend, reaches a road.

6. Cross the road going left and almost immediately on your right is your footpath going by the side of a house and into a field. Keep a straight line along the edge of that field and across the middle of the next field. Head for a gap in the hedge, slightly right, where there is a waymark and gate. Go through and turn right, and aiming for the roof of a house come to a footpath sign in front of the house. Drop to the road, turn right and look for a footpath on your left going up the drive of a house. As the drive turns right, you go straight on for about 100 yards, through kissing gates, eventually reaching a village path. Turn left to gain Weston Church (2.4 miles).

In the churchyard is the famous grave of the giant Jack-o-Legs. The legend states that he was a robber of travellers and that the men of Baldock finally caught him near their town and, before they slew him, they granted his request that they would bury him where an arrow, which he shot from his bow, fell. The arrow soared three miles to Weston and glanced off the church tower to rest where you now find his giant grave.

7. Go through the church gate and turn right onto another clear path. From this path take the second footpath on your left.
(*To reach Weston and its pubs continue along the path for 500 yards. Return to the last spot to continue your walk*).

Keep straight along this path, through a small wood and out, on rising ground, across an open field. Cross a drive and go left and under a large chestnut tree. Go straight across this field heading slightly left to a metal fence, follow it until a kissing gate lets you onto a drive; cross it and follow a wood on your left. Look for a kissing gate near two large trees. Now keep an eye out for other gates or stiles ahead of you but slightly left, until you finally come out onto a road at a very sharp corner.

8. Go straight ahead. The road very soon turns sharply right and even sooner turns sharply left; at this point go straight on, keeping a straight line with a fence and trees on your right. 800 yards from the road you will reach some converted barns (with pond) on your immediate right (Tilekiln Farm). Follow the drive with a right turn to the road in front of the farm. Turn left onto it.

9. Follow the road for 500 yards. A wood will appear on your left. Where a wood starts on your right look out for double gates and a footpath sign. Turn right at this sign and follow this track until you come out onto a road with a ruined church opposite.

Ruined church, Chesfield

This is the Church of St Etheldreda and was the centre of the village of Chesfield. In the late fourteenth century, the parsons from the parishes of Graveley and Chesfield are reputed to have met and fought, presumably because of a dispute over tithes. The vicar of Chesfield lost his life and the parishes were amalgamated a few decades later. Some of the stones of this church were used to repair St Mary's, Graveley. Chesfield is now one of the many deserted villages of Hertfordshire. This village is now only represented by a farm and a few scattered houses.

10. At this point turn left and in 100 yards, at a T-junction, turn right with the ruin on your right. Follow this road; there is a sharp left bend and then a sharp right bend. At this second bend, you must leave the road and go straight on.
The area is threatened with more housing. If this has happened, an alternative route is to follow the road downhill to Graveley Church.
As you follow this track you can see pylons ahead; beyond them the large building in the distance is the Lister Hospital in the town of Stevenage.

Stevenage (which was set up after the Second World War) was the first of the new towns circling London. It is still expanding with a wide range of industry stretching along the A1(M) Corridor. Any aircraft you may see ahead of you, moving from left to right, are on the approach to Luton Airport.
This area is known as Forster Country after E M Forster who grew up in Rooks Nest House. He loved this area and set 'Howards End' here.

Forster Country

11. Before you reach the pylons look for a signpost pointing right. Take this footpath through the middle of a large field with the pylons dropping away to your left. When you come to a hedge keep it on your right (waymarked). Keep straight on until you reach a large hedge across your path. Turn right along it (waymarked), keeping straight on until you turn left onto the road. When this road turns left continue forward and make for Graveley Church (9.4 miles). (*To reach Graveley and its pubs, continue along the road for 400 yards.*)

Graveley Church and the nearby 17th century Graveley Hall and Church Manor are well worth a look.

12. As you pass the church (on your left) the farm track branches into two, take the left one but immediately leave the track for a footpath on your left. After 100 yards, the path turns left; follow a hedge on your left, steadily climbing. There is a small private airfield on your right. Keep straight on through a fruit farm, keeping to the track, with the noise of the A1(M) traffic ahead of you. As the track starts to turn right, look for a gap on the left (unwaymarked) through a hedge and thicket, leading immediately down steps, to the B197. Take care, there is no pavement at the bottom of the steps. Take the road almost opposite and go under the A1(M) turning immediately right onto a gravel track. In about 400 yards, you have a choice. The Hertfordshire Way goes left on a well used permissive path. If you want to go to Letchworth via Willian, continue on this track.

13. This permissive path takes you to the road where you can turn left to Great Wymondley. However, the road is narrow with bends so it is safer to turn right up a field edge for 100 yards to a crossing point then left down another field edge to that road where it is wider so safer. A short road walk gets you to Great Wymondley (11.5 miles). Look for the Green Man pub on your right. Opposite it is a footpath, take it to the church (keep to the left of a double garage up a narrow path).

A lot of research has been done on the archaeology of the village where a Roman villa and cemetery have been discovered. Near to the church there are outlines of two fields, which are of a size allocated to retired Roman army veterans (when they retired they had a right to a certain area of land in the conquered territories). The church has some Norman features. Not on the route but just outside the village stands Delamere House, a red-bricked Tudor building, once the property and residence of Cardinal Wolsey. On his death bed, after his fall from grace with Henry VIII, he said 'Had I but served God as diligently as I have served the King, he would not have given me over in my grey hairs.' On the walk, just after we leave the church on our left is the site of a medieval castle. A little further on the walk is the village of Little Wymondley which has a fine 17th-century timber-framed hall with a fine cluster of chimneys.

Great Wymondley grave

14. Cross the churchyard with the church on your left, and close to a roofed gate on the right, take the footpath ahead across a large field travelling diagonally to the left. Find a pond by the hedge and go through a kissing gate to the left of it into another field. Turn right and cross the next two fields, keeping your direction ahead to a gate road, with farm buildings on the opposite side. Turn right on to the road and go under the railway (this is the East Coast, London to Edinburgh main line).You are now in the village of Little Wymondley (12.2 miles).

Leg 3 Little Wymondley to Codicote

Length 9.3 miles.
Start Little Wymondley, SG4 7HY, TL 215274. Street Parking only
Finish High Street, Codicote, SG4 8XY, TL 215183. free car park at recreation ground TL 217187.
Maps Explorer 193, 182, Landranger 166.
Public Transport Little Wymondley, local bus from Hitchin or Stevenage. Codicote has local buses connecting with surrounding towns.
Pubs/Refreshments Little Wymondley (two), Titmore Green, Chapelfoot on the B656, St Paul's Walden, Whitwell, Codicote has pubs, shops and refreshments at a garden centre.

The Route
This is an excellent scenic leg, quite hilly, with some fine villages and farmland. There are associations with Cardinal Wolsey, and with the late Queen Mother. It is also a well wooded route with areas of parkland. It has some outstanding view points on a clear day, so be on the lookout and not just mile crunching! With so many pubs, this is a good walk to do on a hot day!

The Walk
Before you start the walk, please be warned that at paragraph 2, there is a fast dual carriageway, with a central reservation, to cross. If you have any doubts about your ability to cross this road take this 1-mile detour as follows (all road walking). With the Bucks Head pub on your left walk until you come to a crossroads, turn left and follow this road (no footpath) to the next junction. Turn left again into Titmore Green and when you reach the Hermit of Redcoats on your left, you take the footpath opposite the pub.

1. In the village of Little Wymondley take the footpath beside the Bucks Head pub, through its car park. Follow the climbing footpath through a kissing gate until a water tower comes into view at a second kissing gate.

2. Do not take the track to the water tower, but walk between the tennis courts and pavilion. Cross the playing field with the hedge on your left to a kissing gate.

Soon you will begin to drop to the dual carriageway for the road crossing. (**Cross with extreme care).**
Carry straight on and reaching the road, turn right. On reaching the Hermit of Redcoats pub, take the footpath opposite.

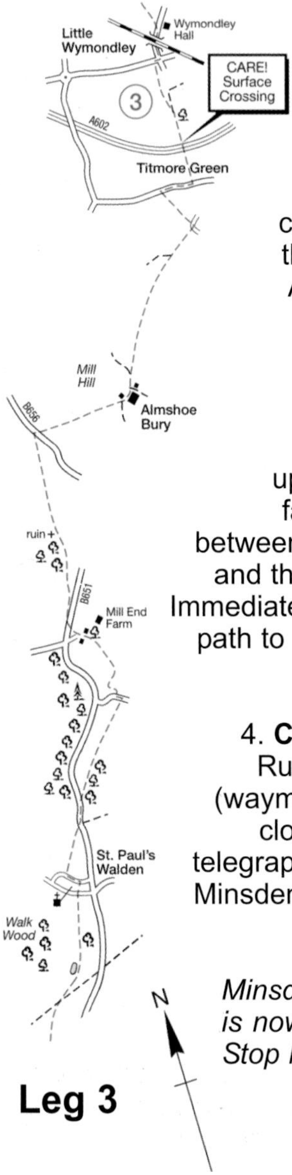

3. Cross the field keeping beside the hedge on the left. On entering the next field (do not go onto the road at the hamlet of Lower Titmore Green) turn 90 degrees and keep the hedge on your left and follow it until you come to a kissing gate. Cross to a second kissing gate and continue with the hedge on your right. When the hedge turns right you carry on across the field heading for a farm on the skyline (this path may not be well walked). As you near a line of hedging, aim for its right corner and a white topped way post. "Within 10 yards of that corner there are steps up through the hedge. Follow this in a straight line, keeping the farm ahead of you, until you reach a farm track, which you take steadily upwards, to the farm (Almshoebury). When the farmhouse becomes visible, take the right fork between the farm buildings. Go through the farmyard and then behind the building that was on your right. Immediately beyond the buildings, take the waymarked path to the right, leading downhill across fields. The path comes out onto a busy road (2 miles).

4. **Cross the road with care** and turn right to the Rusty Gun. At the pub turn left go and up a path (waymarked) between the pub and a shed. Walking close to the hedge on your left, follow the line of telegraph posts upwards. Climb steadily to the ruin of Minsden Chapel, which is hidden behind the trees on the right at the top of the hill.

Minsden Chapel held its last wedding in 1738 but it is now fenced off as it is in a dangerous condition. Stop here to see the excellent views.

Leg 3

You will now start to drop steadily on a clear path to a road. Crossing the road to a footpath diagonally opposite, follow a climbing path until you reach a road; keep straight on with houses on both sides (Langley End). When the road turns left, leave it for a footpath straight ahead. Keep a hedge on your right, and where the track turns left, go straight ahead and drop down through trees to another road.

5. Cross, and go through a kissing gate into a field and follow a footpath across the field. When you reach a wood on your left keep straight on across a field and through a small wood to the road. **Cross with care** and turn left along the road for 200 yards. **This is a dangerous, twisting road with no footpath**. It will take you past the gated entrance to the Sue Ryder Home on your right; continue on the road and look (with relief) for a footpath on the right and take it. Follow the path to the telegraph pole and continue with a field edge and then fencing on your left. On coming to a minor road, turn left and then right into the churchyard of St Paul's Walden (4.3 miles).

St Pauls Walden memorial to the Queen Mother

The church will repay a visit. It has an unusual interior with an English Baroque chancel (the part in front of the altar). It was designed and built in 1727 by Edward Gilbert, with a barrel vaulted ceiling and painted plaster walls. The late Queen Mother was baptised here in 1900 and there is a memorial to her in the churchyard.

6. Follow the track downhill. At the bottom you will pass a house with ornate windows on your left and a little further on you will catch glimpses of St Paul's Walden Bury to your right, the house where the late Queen Mother was reputedly born.
The grounds are occasionally open to visitors, and well worth a visit.
You are now on a private drive to the Bury and where it turns right towards the house, go through a kissing gate on your left. Care: take the left hand path, and keeping the fence on your left, slowly drop down to an access farm road. (If you turn right here and walk through the farm buildings you will find the delightful 'Emily's Tearooms'). Cross the farm access road, walk down to the river, cross it, and go into the village of Whitwell (5.2 miles).

The village was once part of the more important St Paul's Walden but outgrew its parent though it is still part of the Parish of St Paul's Walden. The High Street is lined with an interesting blend of half-timbered Elizabethan houses, brick fronted Georgian houses and Victorian villas. It has a pub and some shops.

7. Turn right into the village and shortly look out for a footpath on your left between houses; take this footpath uphill. When you arrive at an open field, turn left, and almost immediately right alongside a tree.

Having partly crossed this field you will come to a telegraph post and meet a footpath. Turn left on to this path, heading for a line of hedging and look for a mobile phone mast in the distance. Walk towards the mast, and then drop down to a hedge.

8. Start to climb, going slightly right on a clear path.
If the farmer has not reinstated the path head towards a telegraph pole on your right but keep about 25 yards to the left of it. Look back for some fine views.
Over the ridge you drop to a hedge passing between two large trees.Turn left on a track towards a barn, which you pass on your left. After a house on your left, turn left across a drive and look for a footpath on your immediate right. Go through the gate and across the field.

9. Pass through another gate continue ahead keeping fenced off woodland on your right until you until you pass to another field with the hedge now on your left. A wood is now on the hedge side and when you reach the end of it, go through the kissing gate and drop slightly left to a drive. Turn right onto the drive and go over an historic bridge.

Bridge, Hoo Park, Codicote

Notice you have been walking in old parkland and below the bridge is the dried up bed of an ornamental lake.

View from St Pauls Walden

10. Continue until you meet a road, turn right and almost immediately go off on a track on the right. Walk across the field to an access road; continue forward with a small wood on your right hand side. At Rye End Cottages, take the left fork and follow the track keeping the River Mimram on your right. On reaching a road, turn right and continue along it for about 100 yards. Just ahead of you is Kimpton Mill (7.1 miles), but before it, you will turn left onto a bridleway. Keep the river below you on the right. When you come to a wood, leave the main track to take a narrow path climbing steeply left into the wood. Turn left to some half hidden steps on your left. If you miss them, retrace your steps until you find them. At the top of the steps, carry on through the wood, and then through a gate into an open field. You now cross several fields bearing slightly right all the time, through several gates and approaching the woods on your right. You enter the woods and quickly drop to a road.

11. Turn left along the road to the junction and right at the junction. After 100 yards, keep a look out for a signpost on your right. Take this path through the trees until you come to open fields; follow this to a white bungalow (an old gatehouse). This brings you out on a road. (There is a garden centre about 200 yards to your left with a cafe). Turning right for 200 yards takes you into the centre of Codicote where there are shops and pubs (9.3 miles).

Leg 3 (continued)
St. Paul's Walden
Walk Wood
N
B651
River Mimram
Whitwell
B656
4
Codicote
Sch
River Mimram

Leg 3

Leg 4 Codicote to St Albans Roman Museum

Length 12.6 miles.
Start High Street, Codicote, TL 215183. Free car park at recreation ground, SG4 8XY, TL 217187.
Finish St Albans Roman Museum, AL3 4SW, TL 136074. Pay car park.
Maps Explorer 182, Landranger 166.
Public Transport Codicote (see Leg 3). St Albans has national trains and buses.
Pubs/Refreshments Ample on route (see route description).

The Route

We taste a little literature and theatre on part of this walk when we visit the village in which George Bernard Shaw lived (his house now belongs to The National Trust). We see parklands and ruined churches on the way, prehistoric sites and finally the historic town of St Albans – a feast indeed!

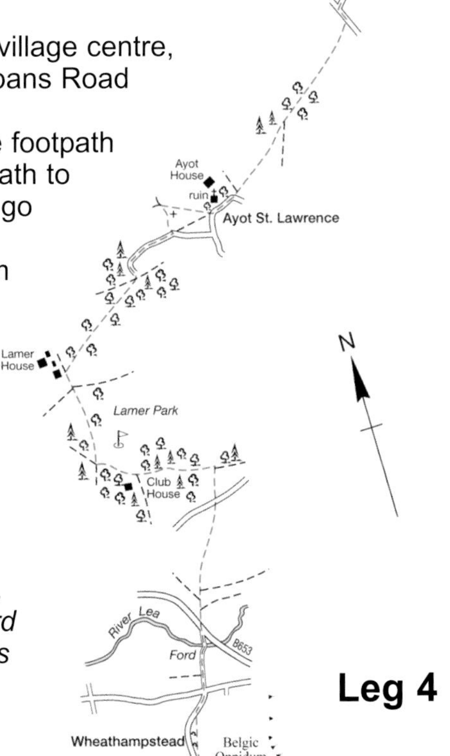

The Walk

1. Start in Codicote High Street village centre, at the traffic lights, take the St Albans Road (opposite Codicote Butchers). In approximately 250 yards take the footpath on the right. Proceed along the path to wooden steps, cross a track and go down another set of steps to a road. Turn left to Codicote Bottom Farm and left again. In approximately 100 yards take the right hand footpath by Ayot Lodge. Ahead of you, a footpath runs alongside a fence, which eventually leads to the gates of Ayot House. Go out of the gates and turn right through Ayot St Lawrence (1.8 miles).

In the village there is a lot to see. The house where George Bernard Shaw lived and wrote many of his great plays is now owned by the National Trust and well worth a visit.

There is a ruin of the church pulled down by Sir Lionel Lyde to be replaced by a classically styled building in its own park. Ayot House is a Queen Anne style building built on to the basic Tudor manor house where William Parr, brother to Catherine, Henry VIII's last Queen, lived.

Palladian Church, Ayot St Lawrence

2. Go past the pub (Brocket Arms) on your left and the ruined church on your right taking the footpath by the side of the white cottage (Ruins Cottage). Cross the meadow by the right hand path to the new church. *This was built to fit in with the style of the 'grand' house and is worth a visit.*

Go round the side of the church to a drive, turning left with the church on your left. When you come to a road turn right and follow it to the second footpath on the left at a bend in the road.

Go through a gap in the fence. Follow the footpath through a wooded area, ignore a minor track that crosses the path, continue on through an avenue of trees and at the second kissing gate turn left. After a few yards you will pass Lamer House on the right. After a further 75 yards keep left leaving the metalled road. Continue for 400 yards then turn left via a kissing gate. Walk between two wire fences. When the path divides keep left and continue with a wire fence to your left.

On reaching a kissing gate turn right and follow the footpath to a road. Cross the road to the path opposite, follow down the path and under a bridge to a ford. Follow through to a road and cross to Dyke Lane. We are now on the edge of Wheathampstead (4.4 miles).

Bluebells in Devil's Dyke

Devil's Dyke is a great prehistoric earthwork. Look out for a plaque. This earthwork is part of an Iron Age settlement of the Belgae Tribe (known to the Romans as the Catuvellauni). They ruled large parts of Hertfordshire and were conquered by Julius Caesar when he stormed their capital, Oppidum, in 54 B.C. The capital has been associated with this structure, so you are probably on the site of a great battle fought by the famous Roman General and Emperor.

3. Walk along Dyke Lane until you reach Devil's Dyke on the left. Pass along the bottom of the Dyke to reach wooden steps on the right.. At the road turn left, then follow the road to Beech Hyde Farm, turning left through the farm until you reach a side road where, 40 yards to your right, you take a field path and go through light woods to Coleman Green and the John Bunyan pub (5.5 miles).

Nearby is a house chimney stack, just north of the pub, all that is left of a house where, by tradition, John Bunyan is said to have preached and occasionally to have lived. The house was demolished in 1877 when a plaque was placed there.

4. At Coleman Green follow the path through woodland to reach a road, cross to find two paths, take the right one to Titnol's Wood. Turn right onto a path on the edge of the wood to a stile. Cross the stile and proceed towards houses and a road. Take care as the road is narrow and the verges are steep. Turn right down the road passing a road joining from your right. Ignore a footpath on your left. You then pass a footpath on your right and Hammond's Farm. After 600 yards the road takes a sharp turn to the right. Take the footpath to the left, soon coming to the edge of a wood, which the path enters but stays along its edge.
From this point until we reach the railway line beyond Sandridge the Woodland Trust has bought nearly 1000 acres of land to the right of our footpath which they are turning into a patchwork of woods, glades and farmland with paths for walkers.
Follow this route to the edge of Sandridge. Cross a road and follow a path between gardens, keeping a look out for a path on your left into the churchyard of the ancient parish church (7.8 miles).
The church, built of stone, is one of the most ancient in Hertfordshire, having been founded early in the twelfth-century as a chapel by the abbots of St Albans, and much of the original early Norman work remains. The Chancel was built about 1400. The tower, which has a broad spire, dates from 1887; the original one collapsed in 1688.The interesting feature of the interior is the fourteenth-century stone-built chancel screen, consisting of a central doorway with three windows on each side and a double one over the doorway; the carving on the screen is very fine. The arch is built of Roman brick, probably from the ancient city of Verulamium. Outside, on the S. wall of the chancel, is a scratch sundial. It is recorded that the churchyard held several interesting epitaphs.

"Farewell vain world, I've had enough of thee,
And no't I care not what thou say'st of me,
Thy smiles I court not, nor thy frowns I fear,
I rest in peace, my head lies quiet here."

And over the grave of one who was sexton for 43 years, is this:

"For many years I added dust to dust,
Ashes to ashes, in my neighbours' graves,
Now, Lord, my dust and ashes I entrust
To Thee whose death from death eternal saves."

5. Leave the church by the lych gate. Cross the High Street and turn left along the street. Look out for a sign pointing to Spencer Playing Field. Enter the playing field by the side of the village hall.
Keep the playing field on your left. When you leave the playing field take the left hand path, which follows the telegraph posts. Cross over a minor road (Sandridgebury) and continue to follow the path and soon you will cross over a main line railway into a farmyard. Go through the farmyard and take the farm road (which goes to the right) soon coming to the A1081 (9.6 miles). Cross the road with great care and turn right and follow the main road for about 300 yards.

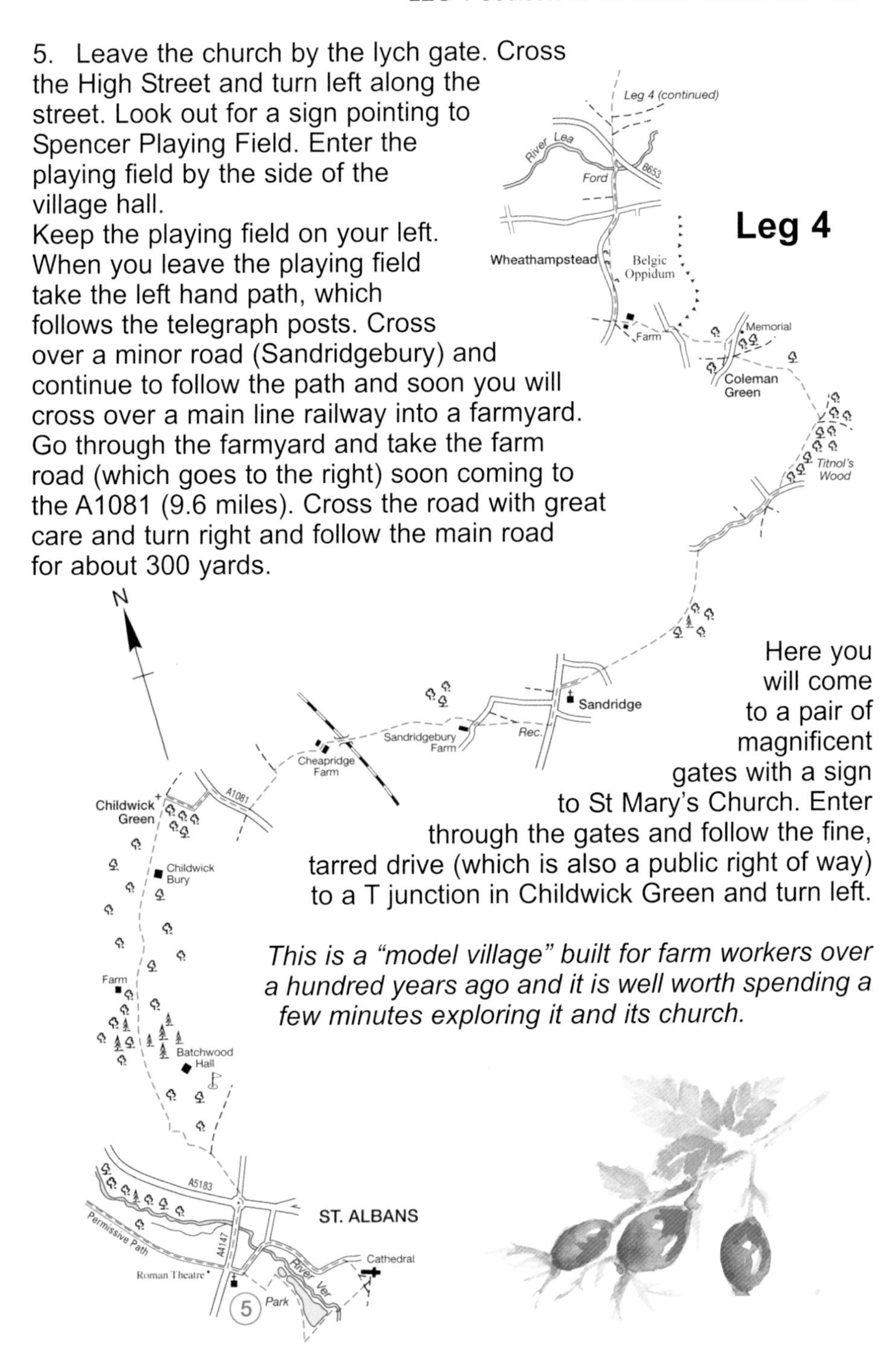

Here you will come to a pair of magnificent gates with a sign to St Mary's Church. Enter through the gates and follow the fine, tarred drive (which is also a public right of way) to a T junction in Childwick Green and turn left.

This is a "model village" built for farm workers over a hundred years ago and it is well worth spending a few minutes exploring it and its church.

6. Pass through the village keeping to the drive (ignore all the private keep out notices – these apply to the land around and not to the drive). Follow this fine section of the walk through old parkland and past the mansion – Childwick Manor. About 800 yards after the house the drive turns to the right; leave the drive at this point and follow the path with high hedges on each side (noticing the goat farm to your left). Cross a field before a golf course appears on your left. After another half mile you come to a road from the golf club. Turn right on to it and follow it to the public road (Batchwood Drive). Cross the road and turn right. After 30 yards you reach the busy Redbourn Road. Cross with great care.

7. After crossing the road go straight on into Bluehouse Hill passing over the little River Ver. Take the first turning on the left. Go about 200 yards, then fork right past the Roman Museum into the car park (12.6 miles). The city centre is 15 minutes away and the trains 25.

Important note
At the beginning of the next leg there is a very special 35 minute "loop walk" around the important sites of St Albans. If you wish, you can do the "loopwalk" at the end of this walk.

St Albans skyline

Leg 5 St Albans to Markyate

Length 11 miles.
Start St Albans Roman Museum, AL3 4SW, TL 136074. Pay car park.
Finish Markyate, AL3 8LJ, TL 062164. Car park in town centre.
Maps Explorer 182, Landranger 166.
Public Transport St Albans (see Leg 4). Markyate has local bus services, which include Dunstable and St Albans.
Pubs/Refreshment Redbourn at TL 111117 (just off your route) and in Flamstead (2).

The Route

This includes a "loop" around the sites of St Albans.

For those who like history and our English heritage this is for you. The town will repay time spent in it, with good shops and lots of history. St Albans is named after the first British martyr who was executed on the site of the Abbey, outside the Roman town, by the Roman authorities in A.D.209. The Roman town (Verulamium) lies just south of the city. It has a good museum, (we start here), hypocaust in situ, a Roman theatre and sections of the city walls. The magnificent Norman and Medieval Abbey (built largely of bricks taken from the Roman city) is worth a visit. There are two other museums. Don't forget when you visit the Abbey to leave a generous donation in the box as the building receives no state subsidy and whatever your religious belief the building needs to be preserved for future generations to enjoy. Added to this you will walk over a buried Roman city and three fine settlements en route. Add a small river, water mills and some fine scenery, and you have it all!

The Walk

1. "The St Albans Loop" Go towards the toilets from the car park and turn right along the path heading to the lake on your left. Follow the lake with it on your left. After about 300 yards climb up the slope on your right (at this point look down on the lake and beyond to the Abbey on its hill) and follow the remnants of the Roman City wall (almost 2000 years old) until you come to a path. Turn right and go 100 yards to admire the outline of the once magnificent London Gate of the Roman City and more of the wall.

Through this gate the first British Christian martyr St Alban – said to be a Roman Officer – was led out of the city, taken over the river to where the abbey now stands, to be executed.

Leg 5

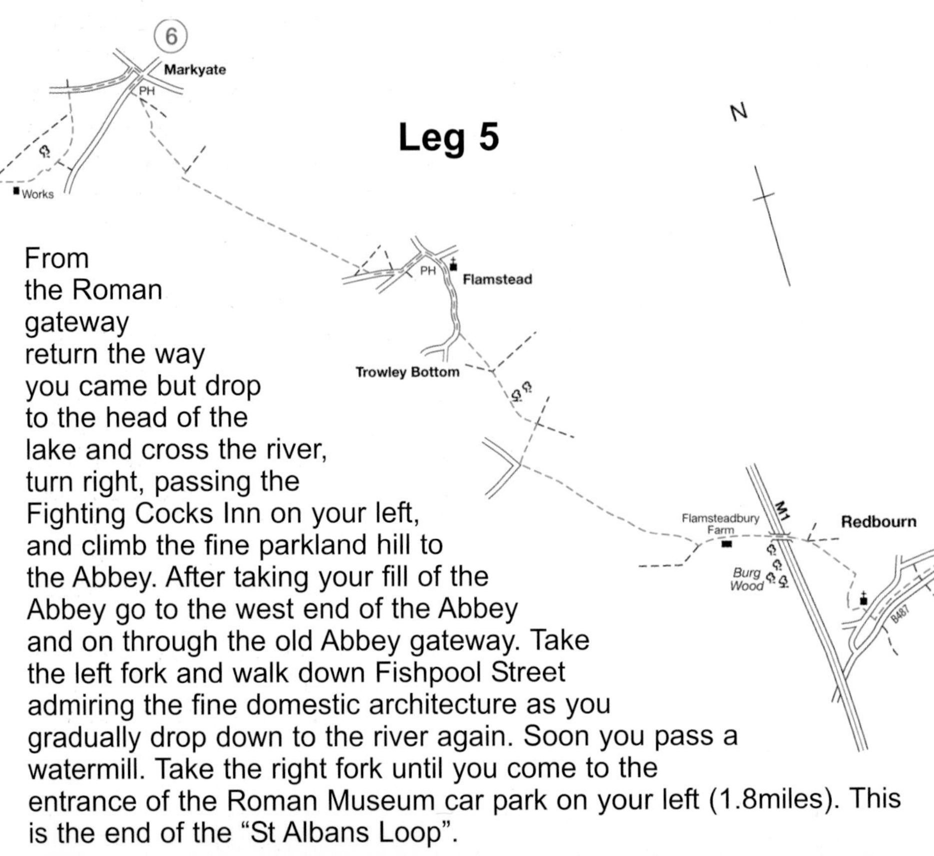

From the Roman gateway return the way you came but drop to the head of the lake and cross the river, turn right, passing the Fighting Cocks Inn on your left, and climb the fine parkland hill to the Abbey. After taking your fill of the Abbey go to the west end of the Abbey and on through the old Abbey gateway. Take the left fork and walk down Fishpool Street admiring the fine domestic architecture as you gradually drop down to the river again. Soon you pass a watermill. Take the right fork until you come to the entrance of the Roman Museum car park on your left (1.8miles). This is the end of the “St Albans Loop”.

Roman Wall, St Albans

2. From this point go to the main road and cross by the controlled crossing. Go into the gates of the lodge of the Gorhambury Estate. (At this point is a notice saying Roman Theatre). The next part is a permissive path and not a right of way and from time to time is closed for estate management purposes. If you are unfortunate and find it closed then go as follows: having crossed the main road turn right. At the roundabout turn left along A5183 and carefully walk to Bow Bridge where you can resume the route.

If you are on the permissive route you are walking over the buried ruins of the Roman City and approximately along the line of the main Roman road. The line of trees ahead of you that crosses your path is roughly the site of the walls and city gate. After 0.8 miles from leaving the main road take the turning on the right (it has a waymark). You will soon cross the River Ver (there is a building on the side of the bridge). Turn left here and follow the river closely upstream until you meet the main road at Bow Bridge (3.3 miles).

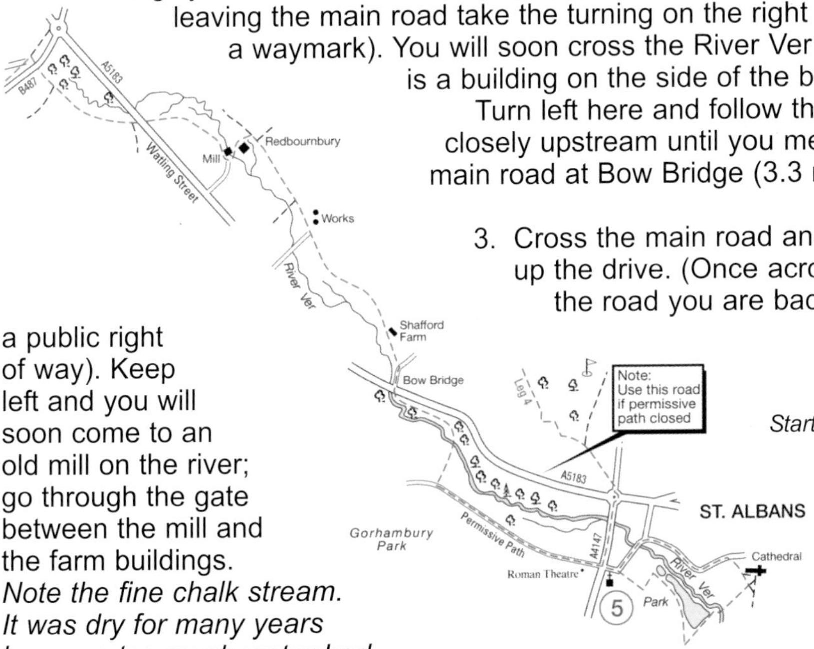

3. Cross the main road and walk up the drive. (Once across the road you are back on a public right of way). Keep left and you will soon come to an old mill on the river; go through the gate between the mill and the farm buildings.
Note the fine chalk stream. It was dry for many years because too much water had been extracted from the underlying chalk by water companies and farmers. Water has been put back into the headwaters and the river has new life.
Soon the track turns uphill to the right but continue straight on by the footpath (as shown by a waymark).When you come to a road, with a waste treatment works in an old quarry, cross the road and follow the waymark, keeping your direction.
Keeping the river on your left you meet a track going off to your right, carry straight on.

At Redbournbury Farm (4.7 miles) cross the river on a footbridge, then cross the mill stream.
On your right is an old water mill, which is being restored, is often open for inspection.
Turn into the mill grounds looking for a footpath left of the mill buildings. The river you were following is now on your right. Follow it to the main road on a clear path.

4. Cross the road, go into the farmyard opposite and look for a kissing gate on your right. Follow this footpath for about a mile until you come to a road on the edge of Redbourn. (*If you turn right at this point there is a pub in about 150 yards*). Cross the road and climb an embankment onto an old railway line. Turn left and follow the bed of the railway. As you walk this old railway track you are going round the edge of Redbourn. In about 0.8 miles look out for Redbourn Church on your right and descend to it.

Redbourn is worth a visit if you have time. Redbourn Common is one of the finest village greens in the country. Cricket has been played here since 1666. Matches are played here every week-end in the season and it holds a cricket week in August. The church has a carved oak screen and some interesting monuments. The main street has a variety of domestic styles and some old coaching inns.

Approaching Flamstead near Trowley Bottom

5. Go through the churchyard with the church on your right (6.2 miles), pass the church tower, come out of the churchyard with the motorway ahead of you and turn right, keeping gardens on your right. Follow the path round, ignoring a footpath going off on your right. Finally cross a

field towards the motorway following a line of telegraph posts. On reaching a road turn left onto it and cross over the M1 motorway. Pass Flamsteadbury Farm on your left and ignore the dirt track on your left; keep to the clear farm road. In a mile there are some large concrete blocks and a road, which at this point turns a sharp corner.

6. At this point turn sharp right off the road onto a bridleway. After about 400 yards look out for a footpath sign on your left and take this route. Drop steeply to the bottom of a valley and carry straight on, ignoring a footpath to the right. When the farm track turns left go straight ahead; soon you will reach a road on the edge of Flamstead. Turn right onto it (Trowley Hill Road) and continue to the village centre (9.3 miles). *Flamstead is a pretty village with pubs and a fine church. Some wall paintings were discovered in the nave (the main body of the church). Among them is a large figure of St Christopher (15th century). Above the chancel arch and in the north east chapel there are scenes of the Last Judgement. Look at the narrow tapering spire, which is known as a "Hertfordshire Spike", a common style in the county. This is a village worth exploring.*

Approaching Markyate

7. Leave the centre of the village on Chapel Road heading north. Turn left into Friendless Lane, then take the right fork, keeping in Friendless Lane and take the second footpath on the right, keeping parallel to some large pylons 300 yards to your left. Keep straight on ignoring all side paths. After crossing a small valley you are joined by a farm road from the left. Keep going straight on with a hedge on your left. When you reach some allotments, go round to the right, and when the path divides keep to the left. On reaching the road, and Markyate, turn right to walk into the centre of this large village (11.0 miles).

Markyate is an old nucleated settlement on the main route from London to the North West. Now that it has a bypass you can enjoy its main street and clustered houses.

Leg 6 Markyate to Tring Railway Station

Length 10.3 miles to Aldbury, 11.4 miles to Tring Station.
Start Markyate, AL3 8LJ, TL 062164. Car park in town centre.
Finish Tring Railway Station, HP23 5QR, SP 951122. Pay car parking.
Maps Explorer 182, 181, Landranger 165, 166.
Public Transport Markyate (see Leg 5). Aldbury has local buses only. Tring Station has national trains.
Pubs/Refreshments No pubs except near end of walk in Aldbury. Café at Monument.

The Route

This is a more wooded section of the walk and we go through part of the Ashridge Estate with its walks, woodland and downland. Again we cross some fine rural scenery. Nearby is the famous Whipsnade Wild Animal and Safari Park. A circular walk could be undertaken to include the park, or a visit to the Safari Park could be arranged by the walker.

The Walk

1. From Markyate High Street walk down Buckwood Road to the end of the houses. Here there is a footpath on your left with a signpost 'Roe End Lane'. Take this path up the hill, with houses on your left, and keep to the field edge, ignoring the path on your right. Continue along the field edge, passing a bench on your right. Pass through the gateway on your left, and the path will take you to Roe End Lane. Turn right into the lane and pass Roe End Farm and continue to Holly Bush Lodge. Turn left onto a wide track and continue, with trees on your right and crops on your left, to Beechwood Home Farm. At this point you come to a cross road of tracks with Kennels Lodge on your left; go left, with the lodge on your immediate right. Continue for 800 yards to Beechwood School.

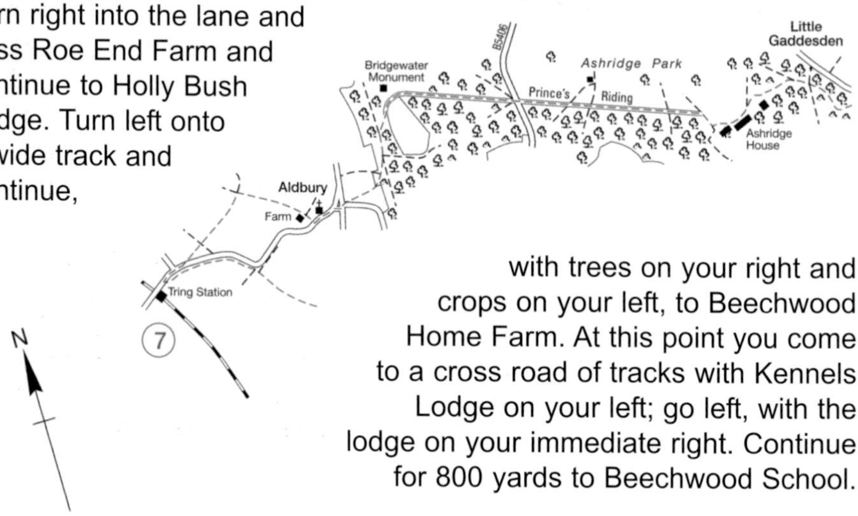

This house was built on the site of a nunnery which, on the dissolution of the monasteries, became a Tudor mansion where Edward VI stayed. The grounds were designed by Capability Brown in 1754 and it became a school in 1964.

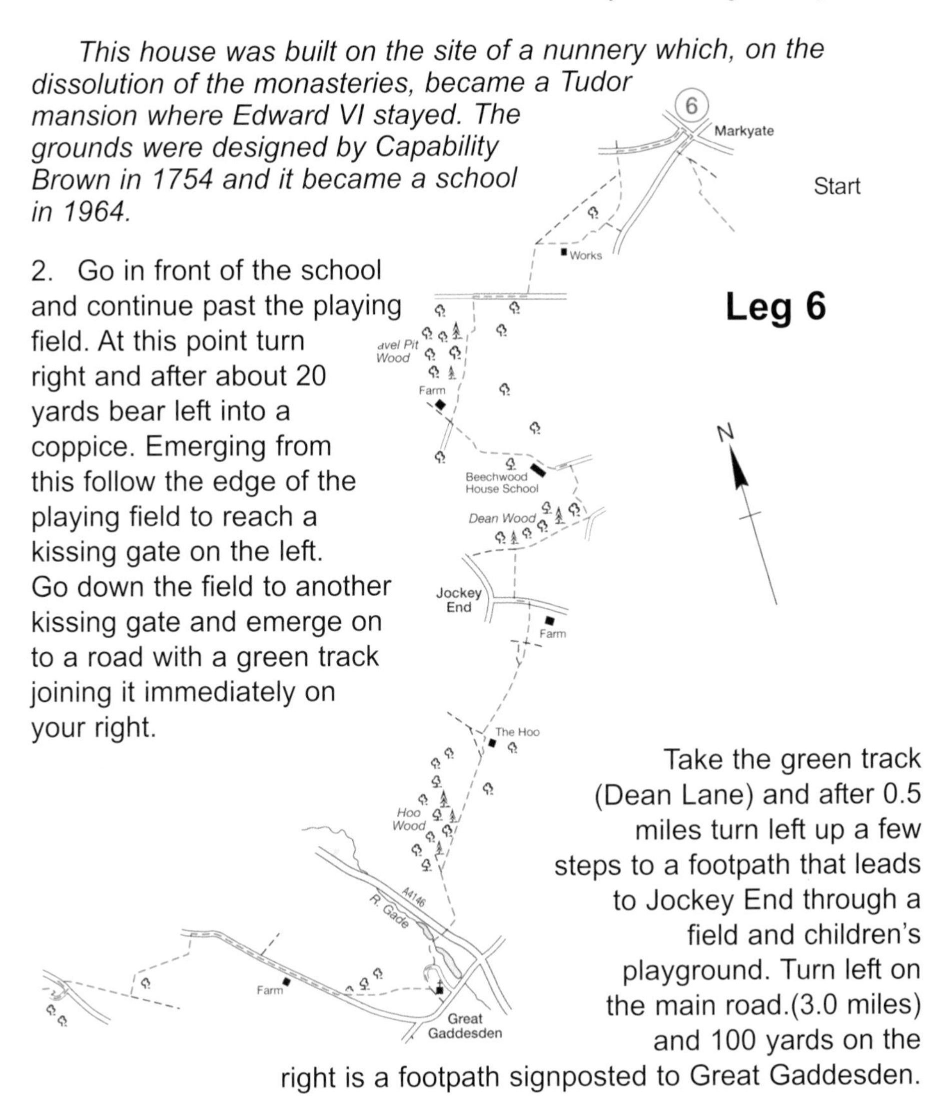

2. Go in front of the school and continue past the playing field. At this point turn right and after about 20 yards bear left into a coppice. Emerging from this follow the edge of the playing field to reach a kissing gate on the left. Go down the field to another kissing gate and emerge on to a road with a green track joining it immediately on your right.

Take the green track (Dean Lane) and after 0.5 miles turn left up a few steps to a footpath that leads to Jockey End through a field and children's playground. Turn left on the main road.(3.0 miles) and 100 yards on the right is a footpath signposted to Great Gaddesden.

3. This route soon opens onto green fields on a clearly marked path. You come to a large house on your left (The Hoo). Pass this house and keep straight on. Soon there is a wood on your right; walk alongside the wood until you can enter the edge of the wood before descending through open fields to the road, with Great Gaddesden beyond. Cross the road and the River Gade, and go towards the village (5.0 miles).

4. Go right into the road named Church Meadows (cul de sac) until you come to a path (near the garages). This path leads diagonally across the fields and through kissing gates to St Margaret's and a road. Turn right onto this road. (There is a Buddhist centre where visitors are welcome). Soon the tarred road peters out and you are on a farm track.

5. After 400 yards there is a footpath bearing half left (just before some houses on your right). It crosses a very large cultivated field into a small valley where it joins another path (still in the large field) coming up the valley from the left. There is a small wood in the field; keep this on your left. Descend into the valley and at the bottom turn right onto the path coming from your left. Follow this path through the kissing gate then diagonally to the road on the edge of Little Gaddesden (7.2 miles).

If you have time a detour into the village is worthwhile and in the church, a little detached from the village, is a memorial to the 3rd Duke of Bridgewater. (See Ashridge).

6. Cross into Cromer Close opposite and onto a path between houses; soon the path turns right and emerges onto a small playing field. Go diagonally to the left and reach a path into the woods. Keep straight on for a short way whereupon a track appears below to the right. Join this track before it swings past a water treatment compound and emerges in the valley bottom onto a gravel track. Go right along this track for 100 yards, where a diagonal grass path crosses; turn left along it up a hill leading into woods. This will shortly reach a wire fence around the Ashridge Centre car park. Follow this up to the front of the house.

We are now on the Ashridge Estate, which covers 4,000 acres of woodland and commons. It is one of the great parks of England. Its origin goes back beyond the Middle Ages and it has developed as fashions in landscaping have changed over the centuries. The estate was acquired by the National Trust in the 1920s and its many acres and miles of paths are open to the public 365 days a year. The area is rich in wildlife. Ashridge House itself started as a monastic establishment in 1276 and lasted until the dissolution in 1535. It was then owned by King Henry VIII and was a country house where the future Queen Elizabeth I stayed. Later it was the home of the Dukes of Bridgewater and the 3rd Duke was the famous Father of Inland Navigation. He built the first canal of the Industrial Age to bring coal from his mines to Manchester (1761).The house today is the result of the Gothic Revival and could be called a romantic Gothic palace with towers, turrets and a spire.

It is now a management college and is not open to visitors, but the immediate gardens are open to the public at certain times.

Prince's Riding and the Bridgewater Monument

7. Walk along the drive in front of the house until the drive reaches a pair of white gates. Cross the small sports field in front of you and head for the metal railings. When you reach these railings, turn left and follow the National Trust footpath around the golf course. Emerging from the wood, you are at the end of a magnificent straight avenue about 1.3 miles long with a tall obelisk at the far end (The Monument). Walk to this obelisk.

The Monument is a Doric column surmounted by an urn and it was erected to the 3rd Duke of Bridgewater. (See the piece on Ashridge). You can climb the monument at certain times on the payment of a fee. There is a National Trust cafe and an excellent information centre, all open at given times (including most weekends).

8. Follow the path in front of the information centre and you begin to drop sharply to the village of Aldbury on a clear path. When you reach the road turn right into the village (200 yards).

Starting the descent to Aldbury

This is a fine village with a green, complete with stocks, and village pond. There are pubs and village shops. There is a range of good domestic architecture. The church has a chapel with an excellent screen separating it from the main church. In the Verney Chapel is the tomb of Robert Whittingham, killed at the Battle of Tewkesbury in 1471.

Aldbury

9. After passing the churchyard (10.3 miles) on your right, look for a footpath on the same side into a field with farm and house buildings on your left. Take this path, crossing the field and passing through the kissing gates to a path, on your left, with a building on one side. You will shortly reach a T junction with a golf course beyond, turn left here and soon come to a road. Keep straight along this road to Tring Station, which is the end of this leg (11.4 miles).

Tring is 1½ miles away from the station. It is an ancient market town located in a valley where the prehistoric Icknield Way crosses the Roman Akeman Street. The Rothschild family lived at Tring Park and the second Baron founded Tring Museum, now part of the Natural History Museum, Kensington. The Tring Reservoirs are an excellent centre for birdwatching. The main railway line was built along the Bulbourne Valley in the 1830s because local landowners opposed the easier eastern route along the Gade valley. The cost of this decision was the major engineering work of Tring Cutting, some 2.5 miles long, which involved the removal of 1.5 million tons of earth.

Leg 7 Tring Railway Station to Kings Langley

Length 15.4 miles which may be taken as two shorter walks.
Leg 7a:Tring Railway Station to either Berkhamsted Railway Station (5.8 miles, paragraphs 1-5) or Hemel Hempstead Railway Station (about 9 miles, paragraphs 1-7a).
Leg 7b: Berkhamsted Railway Station to Kings Langley Railway Station (9.6 miles,paragraphs 6-15) or Hemel Hempstead Railway Station to Kings Langley Railway Station (about 9 miles, paragraphs 7b and 9–15).
Start Tring Railway Station, HP23 5QR, TL 951122. Pay car parking.
Finish Kings Langley Railway Station, WD7 8LF, TL 080020. Pay car parking
Maps Explorer 181, 182, Landranger 165, 166.
Public Transport Tring (see Leg 6). Berkhamsted, Hemel Hempstead and Kings Langley all have train and local bus services.
Pubs/Refreshments Berkhamsted, Bourne End, Little Hay Golf Complex, Bovingdon, Chipperfield.
Car parks Pay car parks at all the stations.

The Route
The route climbs the ridge to return to the Ashridge Estate, encountered on the previous leg. After passing through an extensive stretch of wooded common the route reaches more open common land with far-reaching views, then descends into Berkhamsted with its numerous historic connections. A walk along a largely rural section of canal towpath offers refreshment opportunities in canal-side pubs. From the village of Bourne End the route climbs again, then much of the remainder of the leg is through quiet farmland and the wooded Chipperfield Common. Although a long stage the route is mainly easy going, and includes a section of quiet country lane.

This stage coincides in places with several other way-marked walks. A leaflet describing the Ashridge Estate Boundary Trail may be obtained from the National Trust Visitor Centre (01442 851227); leaflets for the Grand Union Canal Circular Walks and the Chipperfield Common Heritage Trail, as well as more general information, are available from Dacorum Tourist Information Centre (01442 234222); details of The Chiltern Way are available from The Chiltern Society (www.chilternsociety.org.uk).

Much of the Ashridge Estate is common land, over which residents from neighbouring parishes including Berkhamsted, Northchurch, Aldbury, Pitstone and Ivinghoe for centuries exercised their rights to graze animals and collect fuel. In the early 20th century much of this activity gradually declined, then stopped altogether. As a result what was once open heathland with scattered trees has become wooded with naturally regenerated trees and shrubs. There are many public paths through the Estate, but our route is described below.

The Walk

1. From Tring Station turn right on to Station Road. Just beyond the car park turn right through a gate and walk along the footpath that runs along the northern edge of the field.
(*This is not recorded as a right of way on the Definitive Map but has been used by walkers for years*).
On reaching the far corner of the field go south-east on a bridleway with a hedge and telegraph poles on the left. Cross a horse-gallop and leave the field by a short lane with hedges on both sides to reach a road. Cross the road and continue on the bridleway opposite. Go past a large house (Brightwood) and a wall on the right. Continue along the bridleway as it ascends through a tunnel of trees to a signpost. Turn right (south) and follow the footpath along the edge of the wood. The footpath swings left through the wood and continues to climb. Emerge from the wood on a small green edged with bollards. Cross in front of the gates of Tom's Hill House.

2. Enter the woods on the footpath to the left of Tom's Hill House gates. After 150 yards on this path cross a way-marked footpath and after another 70 yards bear right on the main path for a further 300 yards, following the footpath waymarks to a path junction. Bear right onto the Ashridge Estate Boundary Trail (AEBT) and follow this broad track for about a quarter-mile until it forks at a signpost. Take the left fork for 20 yards, then turn sharp left away from the AEBT and walk northeast in a straight line along a broad ride with mature trees on the left. Keep going in the same north-easterly direction along a broad avenue until the road.

3. Emerge at the road by a 'public bridleway' signpost. Turn right along the road to the T-junction (150 yards). Cross this road (B4506) and follow the bridleway in an easterly direction across Berkhamsted Common. At Little Coldharbour Farm join a gravel track leading towards Coldharbour Farm.

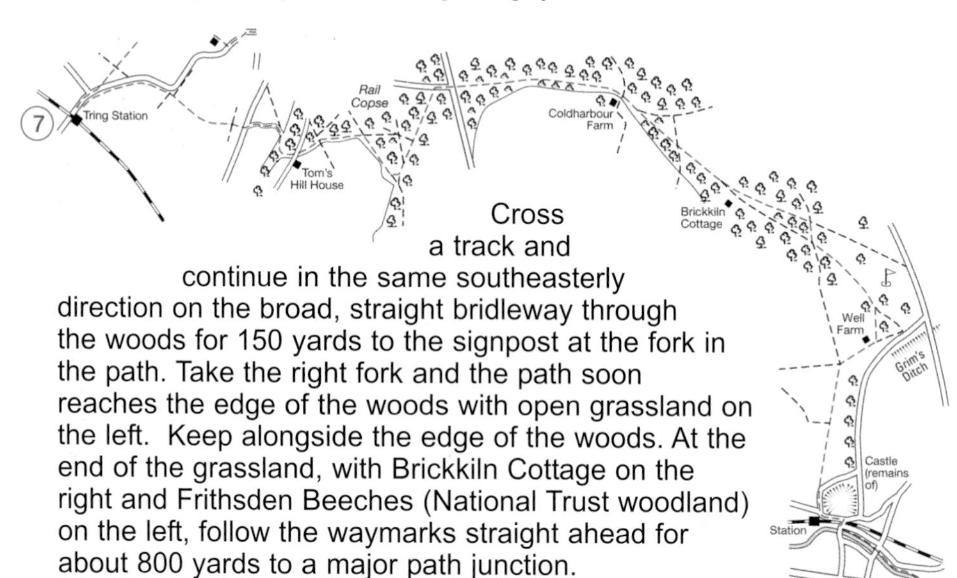

Cross a track and continue in the same southeasterly direction on the broad, straight bridleway through the woods for 150 yards to the signpost at the fork in the path. Take the right fork and the path soon reaches the edge of the woods with open grassland on the left. Keep alongside the edge of the woods. At the end of the grassland, with Brickkiln Cottage on the right and Frithsden Beeches (National Trust woodland) on the left, follow the waymarks straight ahead for about 800 yards to a major path junction.

Berkhamsted Common is mostly owned by the National Trust and is part of the Trust's Ashridge Estate. In 1866 an attempt was made by the then owner, Earl Brownlow, to enclose part of Berkhamsted Common. The railings he put up were removed in a single night by 120 navvies and after a long court battle the commoners' rights were upheld. The estate was later sold to pay death duties and parts of it were acquired by the National Trust in the 1920s. The area is rich in wildlife.

4. At this major path junction turn right (south) and follow the path for about 90 yards to the next signpost. Turn left (southeast) and follow the level path along the Common with views to Berkhamsted on your right. Continue past some restored World War I practice trenches to another path junction. Take the right hand fork and descend for about 200 yards through a wood. Turn right at the next path junction and follow the path out of the woods and along a tarmac lane down the hill to Well Farm. At Well Farm turn left and follow the path along the hedgerow, emerging on Kitchener's Field.

During the First World War, the Inns of Court Officers Training Corps, nicknamed 'The Devil's Own', were billeted on Kitchener's Field and as part of their training dug extensive practice trenches on Berkhamsted Common, prior to being deployed to the western front.

5. Continue straight on past the tennis courts and bowls club on the left, emerging onto Castle Hill, Berkhamsted. Continue straight along Brownlow Road with Berkhamsted Castle on the left.

Turn left (east) onto White Hill and the entrance to the Castle is immediately on the left (5.8 miles).

Berkhamsted Castle is an 11th century motte-and-bailey castle on the site where, in 1066 after the Battle of Hastings, William of Normandy received the crown of England. It is administered by English Heritage and is open to the public at no charge. On a fine day this is a good spot for a picnic lunch.

Berkhamsted Railway Station is just west of the Castle, for those who want a shorter walk with a return to the start point in Tring by train.

6. From the Castle entrance, continue east along the White Hill roadway for about 200 yards and then turn right under the railway and cross the road at The Crystal Palace pub to reach the Grand Union Canal towpath.

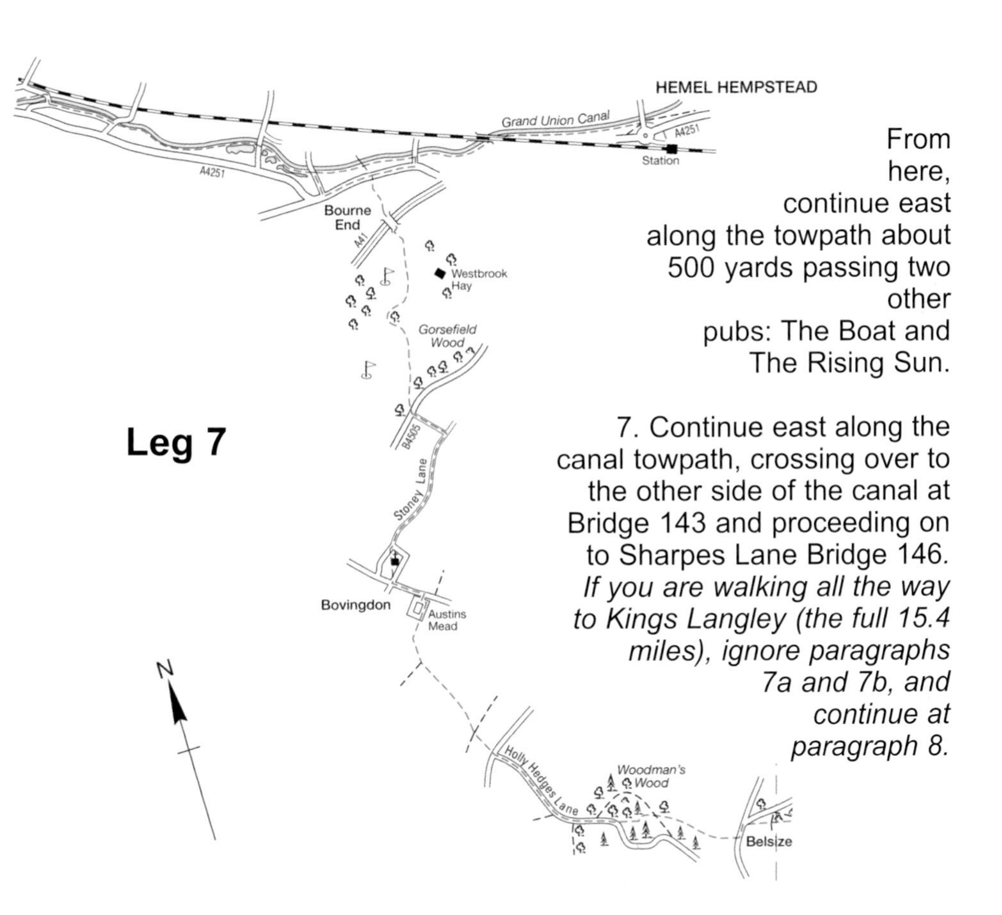

From here, continue east along the towpath about 500 yards passing two other pubs: The Boat and The Rising Sun.

7. Continue east along the canal towpath, crossing over to the other side of the canal at Bridge 143 and proceeding on to Sharpes Lane Bridge 146. *If you are walking all the way to Kings Langley (the full 15.4 miles), ignore paragraphs 7a and 7b, and continue at paragraph 8.*

7a. For the shortened walk to Hemel Hempstead: follow the towpath for another 1.3 miles. At the Fishery Lock, bridge 149, leave the towpath and at the top of the steps turn right then cross the road. Go through the gate on the left to follow the tarmac path across the moor, to another gate opposite the pedestrian crossing over the A4251 immediately in front of Hemel Hempstead Railway Station.

7b. To walk from Hemel Hempstead to Kings Langley: leave Hemel Hempstead Railway Station and cross the A4251 by the pedestrian crossing. Go through the gate opposite to cross the moor by the tarmac path, leave by another gate and turn right towards the Fishery Inn. Almost immediately cross the road and descend the steps to the canal towpath. Head west along the towpath for 1 mile to reach the swing-bridge by the Three Horseshoes pub, then turn left into Winkwell lane. Follow the lane to the main road (A4251), turn right, follow the main road for 350 yards and just before reaching Bourne End village hall on your right hand side, cross the road and go onto the bridleway beside a yellow-brick bungalow. Resume the main walk as described in paragraph 9 below.

Grand Union Canal. Originally called the Grand Junction Canal, it was part of a plan to link the Trent to the Thames. Work began in 1793. The Tring section was opened in 1799, and the whole canal, with 101 locks, was completed by 1805. The Tring Reservoirs were built to supply the canal which is 400 feet above sea level at this point. The canal was renamed the Grand Union after amalgamation with other canal companies in 1929.

8. Leave the towpath, turning right into Sharpes Lane and continue to the London Road (A4251). Turn left, stay this side of the road until you can cross to the pavement opposite and follow the road past Bourne End Lane, the Anchor and the White Horse pubs (7.8 miles). Immediately past a yellow-brick bungalow, opposite Bourne End village hall, turn right along a bridleway.

Bourne End lies at the end of the Bourne Gutter, a tributary of the River Bulbourne. The Gutter is a winterbourne, or stream which tends to flow only following heavy winter rainfall, a typical feature of chalk areas. Occasionally it is full of water for three miles. It is known locally as a 'woe-water' and when it appears it is said to predict disaster or tragedy. More likely this is an indicator that the chalk aquifer is at a high level.

9. The route climbs steadily then crosses the A41 trunk road by a footbridge. At the far end of the bridge there is a signpost pointing the

route of the footpath uphill across the golf course; the path may not be obvious, but the direction of the post accurately indicates the route, which runs up the right hand side of a fairway to a second signpost.

Grand Union Canal at Bourne End

Go straight on, with a green on the left, passing scattered trees, then a spinney, on the right, to join another footpath at a T-junction. A large house, Westbrook Hay which is now a school, is visible on your left. Turn right: this path keeps to the left of the golf course. Ignore the gap to the left and keep straight on. From here there are far-reaching views across the Bulbourne Valley and Berkhamsted.

The path passes two small bungalows on the left, the first almost hidden by trees. It then soon swings to the left, goes round the far side of a large storage shed and joins a metalled road. Go along this road as it swings right round a putting green and passes the red brick and wooden building of the Little Hay Golf Complex.

10. About 100 yards beyond the far side of the golf complex car park bear left from the road onto a footpath (marked by a signpost), which cuts through the edge of Gorsefield Wood, keeping to the right-hand path. Towards the far side of the wood you will see the gate and road ahead where the footpath emerges from the trees. Turn right onto Hempstead Road, then immediately left into Bushfield Road. At the far end of Bushfield Road turn right into Stoney Lane and continue straight ahead along this lane into Bovingdon (10 miles). Enter the churchyard by the lych gate and follow the path past the church to Church Street. Turn right here.

Bovingdon. The present church, rebuilt in 1845 on the site of a 13th century church, contains the medieval tomb of a 14th century knight. It has one of the largest churchyards in the county. In the centre of the village is a pentagonal wooden wellhouse, erected in 1881 in memory of Sir Granville Rider of Westbrook Hay. The village has pubs and other facilities.

11. Turn left and go slightly uphill on Chipperfield Road. After about 300 yards turn right into the second turning into a small housing estate, Austins Mead, at the signpost to Bovingdon Green. At the far end of Austins Mead take the footpath between two houses, go through the kissing gate and keep to the fenced path along the right-hand edge of the field. After the next gate bear left diagonally across the field to the right of the fence and go through another gate. Bear left again on the path between two wire fences. After the next kissing gate go straight on into the next field and keep to the left hand edge of this field with a hedge at your left. Where the hedge turns sharply to the left bear slightly right of your previous direction to go across the middle of an open field towards the row of trees ahead. You will have a large glasshouse on your right. The path continues along the right hand side of the field with a fence and trees on the right. Bear left at the next path junction keeping the hedge on your right. Leave the field, cross the road and continue along Holly Hedges Lane for 800 yards.

12. After passing Hollow Hedge cottage and two other houses on the left, the lane enters Woodman's Wood. Keep to the tarmac for another 300 yards or so, passing a wide gateway on the left. Just after the lane

turns sharply right, take the path signposted "Belsize ¾", into the wood. Where the path crosses another path, keep straight on the left-hand path going slightly uphill. As the path levels out you will have a field then a holly hedge on your left, and the wood on your right. Beyond the wood keep to the left-hand side of the field to go downhill to Dunny Lane. Turn left at the road and after 80 yards or so, at the foot of Windmill Hill, turn right up a bridleway which climbs through the trees of Chipperfield Common (12.8 miles).

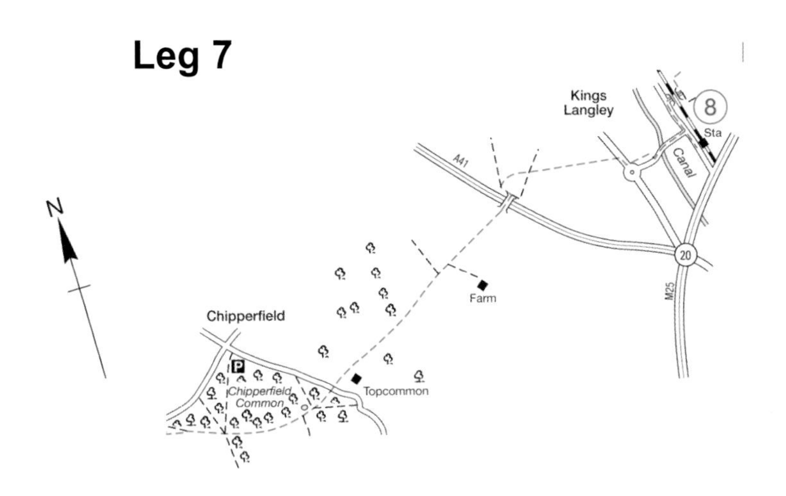

Chipperfield. The village, with its church (1837), cricket field and pubs lies at the northern apex of the common. The wooded common (118 acres) was under royal ownership as part of the Kings Langley estate, until most of the estate was sold to the City of London in 1630 to pay debts owed by Charles I. Later the common was in private ownership until it was given to the then local authority in 1936. It contains two prehistoric burial mounds and a number of ancient sweet (Spanish) chestnut trees said to date from the 1600's. On the southern edge is the Apostles Pond, so called because of the 12 surrounding lime trees planted 1714. In the 1980s the original trees were pollarded, and twelve new trees were planted.

13. There are many paths through the trees across the common; the most direct route (our route) follows the bridleway at the right hand edge of the common with some houses to the right until it reaches the Apostles Pond (0.8 miles). A few paces beyond the pond, with a 6-barred iron gate on your right, bear half left away from the bridleway along a narrow path through the trees.

Apostles Pond, Chipperfield

This path is not very distinct, but goes in a NE direction, soon crossing another wider path. Keep going in a NE direction, to cross a broad bridleway and emerge from the common at Top Common by a signpost to “Kings Langley 1½”.

Descent from Topcommon

14. Cross the road and enter the footpath between wooden fences to the left of the entrance drive for Top Common. In quick succession the footpath goes through four kissing gates, and then follows the left hand edge of a field between fences, goes through another kissing gate and then descends the left hand edge of the next field. At the bottom of the descent the path goes straight on through another gate and ascends a gentle slope along the right hand edge of a field. At the next gate continue straight on but with the hedge on your left, then at the next set of gateways continue straight again following the signpost to Kings Langley, with the hedge to your right. Keep going straight through three more kissing gates, until the path enters a field.

Here keep going in the same direction towards a gap which is clearly visible in the hedge ahead. Go through the kissing gate and cross this field in the same direction, then turn right at the fence to reach a footbridge.

15. Cross the A41 by the footbridge. At the far side of the footbridge turn left and after about 50 yards go through a kissing gate into a field. Keep to the left hand edge of this field and descend along a broad track which eventually reaches Kings Langley at the Watford Road (A 4251), between Wayside Farm and Cedar Lodge. Turn right along the main road for 100 yards, then left down Station Footpath just before the roundabout. At the bottom of the footpath join the road to cross the canal and continue to the T-junction with Station Road. The entrance to the station car park is directly opposite and Kings Langley Railway Station is about 150 yards to the right along Station Road (15.4 miles). Turn left on Station Road to reach the start of Leg 8.

Kings Langley. Lying in the valley of the River Gade, Langley was held by Robert de Mortain, a half brother of William the Conqueror, in 1086 at the time of the Domesday Book. Queen Eleanor of Castile, wife of Edward I, bought the manor for £20 in 1276, and built a large royal palace here with its own deer park. For nearly two centuries it was a major royal residence. Edward II spent much time there with his notorious friend, Piers Gaveston, and also founded a priory near the palace in 1308. A number of later royal family members spent time at the palace, until it went into decline after a fire in 1431. What little remains of the priory, and the site of the royal palace, are to be found at the top of Langley Hill (TL 065026). The Parish Church of All Saints was founded in the 12th century, although its structure mainly dates from the 15th century. Paper making was already established in the area in the early 19th century when John Dickinson bought two former corn mills on the River Gade and developed the business into a major industrial enterprise. One of Dickinson's mills at Frogmore is the world's oldest mechanised paper mill which still makes paper and is open to the public as part of the Apsley Paper Trail. In 1913 production of Ovaltine started in Kings Langley. Business boomed and a new factory with a striking art deco facade, now residential accommodation, was built in the 1920s - it is located just past the start of Leg 8. To supply the factory Numbers and Parsonage Farms were bought in 1929 and rebuilt as model dairy and poultry farms. Production on the site ended in 2002.

Leg 8 Kings Langley to Shenley

Length 12.3 miles.
Start Kings Langley Station WD4 8LF, TL 080020. Station car park (pay)
Finish Shenley, WD7 9DW, TL 182006. Free car park.
Maps Explorer 182, 173, Landranger 166.
Public Transport Kings Langley (see Leg 7). Shenley, where there are local bus services, is a short walk from the finish. Radlett Station 2.2 miles.
Pubs/Refreshments Round Bush, Letchmore Heath, Shenley Park.

The Route

The most powerful influence on the landscape of southern Hertfordshire is London. Since Roman times, London has been the stimulus for building traffic routes northwards through the county and for the concentration of centres of population within easy travelling distance of the capital. The walk from Kings Langley to Shenley threads its way, mostly along green belt, between the southern edges of Hemel Hempstead and St Albans (to the north) and Abbots Langley and the northern suburbs of Watford (to the south). Although the M25 shares this corridor, and the walk also crosses the M1, the A405 London orbital road and the three main railway lines from London to the north, the traffic and the towns are mostly out of sight, if not always out of ear-shot. Much of the way is through open farmland, parkland and woods.
The original route went through Numbers Farm and stayed on the northern side of the M25 for about 2.2 miles. This new route crosses the M25 soon after the start and re-joins the old route just before the start of Chequers Lane.

The Walk

1. Starting from King's Langley railway station turn right along Station Road. About 250 yards beyond the station turn right into Egg Farm Lane. Go under the railway arch and bear right. (If you are leaving from the station car park you can avoid some road walking by leaving the car park by steps at the far end to reach Egg Farm Lane. Turn right into the lane). Continue along Egg Farm Lane, a private road which is also a footpath, to reach a bridge over the M25 motorway.

Large gates on the right of Egg Farm Lane lead to the offices and tall wind turbine of Renewable Energy Systems. The offices are on the site of the Ovaltine Egg Farm. The Ovaltine factory building can be seen in the valley by looking back as the path approaches the M25 bridge. The factory closed in 2002 and there is now private housing behind the façade. In 1865 a Swiss chemist, George Wander, invented the health drink 'Ovomaltine' containing barley malt, milk and eggs. Wander's son, Albert, took over the firm, and established a small factory in Kings Langley in 1913. He changed the name of the drink to 'Ovaltine' for the British market. The company rapidly expanded and the large Art Deco factory was built between 1924 and 1929. In 1929 Wander bought nearby Numbers Farm and Parsonage Farm, which became known as the Poultry or Egg Farm and the Dairy Farm. The buildings of the Dairy Farm were converted to residential use in the early 1990s. The old Dairy Farm gateway can be seen to the left as the walk emerges into Bedmond Road.

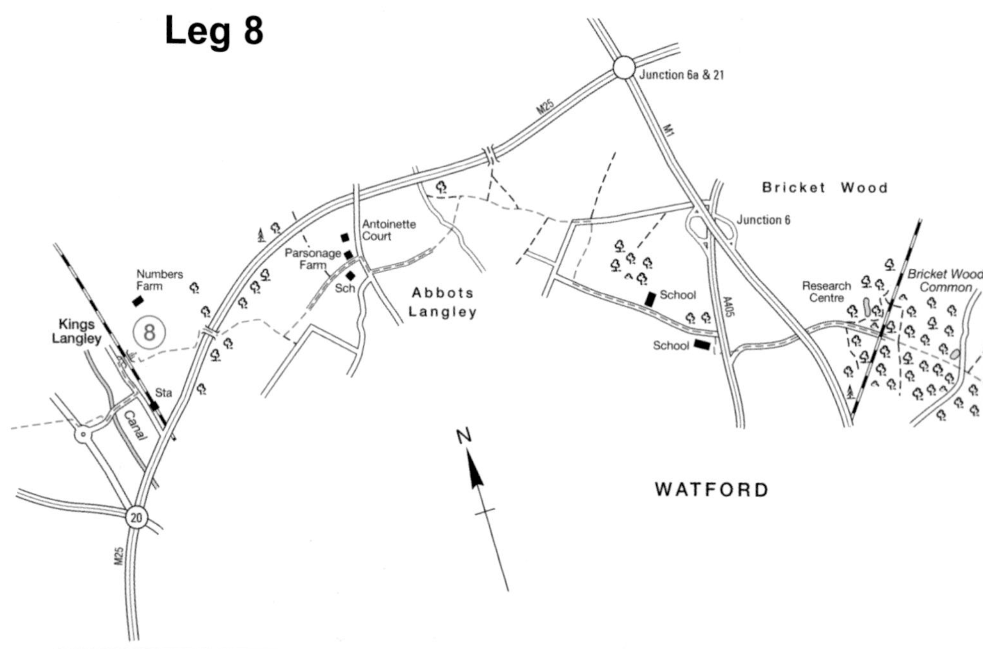

Former Ovaltine factory, Kings Langley

2. Cross the bridge over the motorway and follow the road as it turns left. In 120 yards, where the roadway becomes an unsurfaced track, keep going in the same direction along the public footpath, then after 250 yards turn right onto a path between fields. In 200 yards turn left onto a footpath with mature trees and a hedge on the right. Follow this footpath straight on for 0.5 miles until it joins Bedmond Road. Turn right along the pavement and in 100 yards cross the road at a pedestrian crossing. Continue down Love Lane into a recreation ground. Keep to the left-hand side of the recreation ground and go onto a footpath between hedges. Continue across an open field, through a kissing gate, cross a sunken track, then go ahead on the path as it descends the slope of the next field. Follow it as it turns right at the hedge and in 300 yards it joins a bridleway.

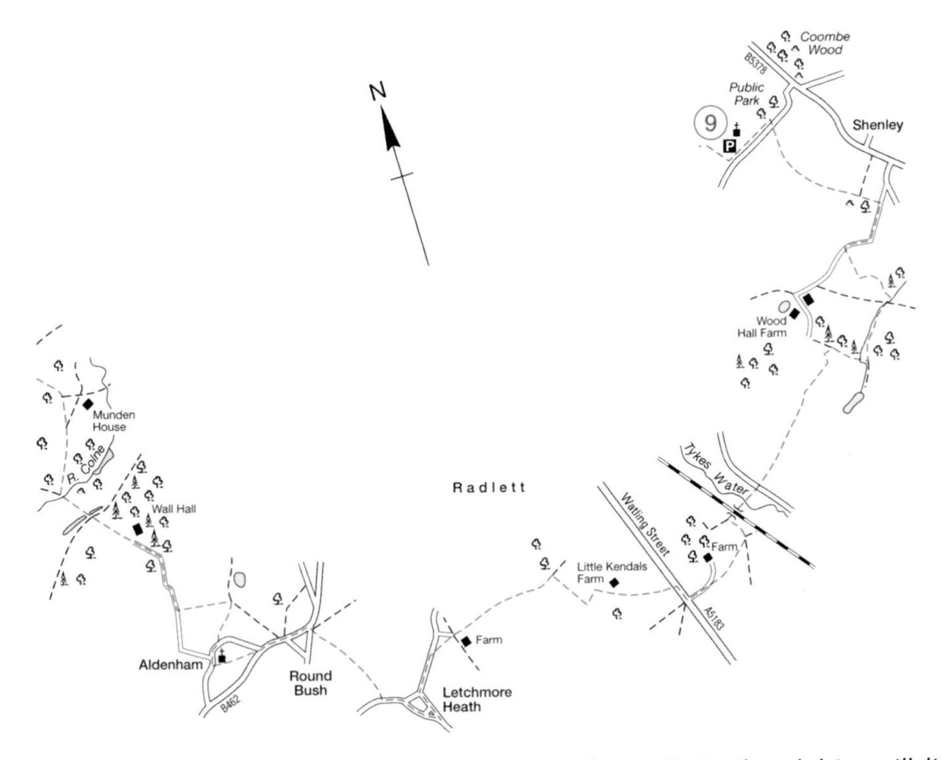

3. Keep along the bridleway, ignoring a footpath to the right, until it joins Chequers Lane at a barrier (2.6 miles). Continue in the same direction along the lane for about 100 yards. Take care, as this is a narrow lane which has quite a steady flow of traffic at times. Take the footpath on the right through a gap in the hedge opposite a lane between cottages (Waterdale Cottage). Continue along the field edge

keeping the hedge on your right then onward between fences past Fortunes Farm until you reach High Elms Lane.

4. Turn left onto a shared footpath/cycle track that runs alongside High Elms Lane passing Parmiter's School and a crematorium on your left. Once past the crematorium cross the road and continue on the footpath along the right hand side to the T junction with the A405. Turn right along the A405 and cross it by a subway. Go up the slope to Bucknalls Lane and turn left along it following the signpost to the Building Research Establishment. Continue along this road across the MI and keep straight on until the road narrows. Take the bridleway to the right into the edge of Bricket Wood Common.
Bricket Wood is a large wooded common where the River Ver meets the Colne. Follow the bridleway straight ahead in a southeasterly direction through the Common.

5. Cross the railway line by a red brick bridge. Cross a signposted footpath and continue to School Lane. Cross this lane and continue through a metal gate near a notice to Munden. Continue along the gravel track. Turn right through a kissing gate into parkland. Cross this diagonally (south) crossing Munden House drive *(Munden House is an*

Wall Hall Mansion

early 19th century Gothic mansion) by a signpost and continuing to an iron footbridge over the River Colne (5.5 miles).

6. Follow the well-trodden path across the field to another footbridge over a gulch. Continue in the same direction with a golf course on the right. Leave the track beside an iron gate. Continue in the same direction on a road through what was Wall Hall grounds, and is now a housing complex.

Wall Hall house was built in 1802 when the Gothic revival style was in fashion. It was then called Aldenham Abbey. A sham ruin was also built, parts of which came from Aldenham Church. Wall Hall became a teacher training college in 1945 and then became part of the University of Hertfordshire before being sold for residential use.

7. At a junction take Wall Hall Drive to the right in front of a black wooden barn and continue in the direction of Aldenham. Turn left on a footpath across a field towards a pylon. Turn right before a kissing gate and continue along the left hand edge of the field.

8. At the end of the field carry on between houses towards the church. Cross the road and enter the churchyard. Follow the path to the right, round the church and on through the churchyard on the south side of the building.

The church of St John is 13th century with numerous later additions. It is partly faced with Hertfordshire pudding stone, a conglomerate stone unique to Hertfordshire. It has a needle spire rising from the centre of the tower roof, well within the parapet; such spires are a peculiarity of the county, and are known as Hertfordshire Spikes.

Where the path turns to the right, keep going straight ahead (east) along a grassy path with a red brick wall on the left. Cross Church Lane and continue along the main road to Round Bush. *The Round Bush pub is down the lane to the right.* Immediately after passing the signpost to Edge Grove School, veer to the right away from the main road, keeping the row of houses on your right. Cross Primrose Lane and enter the field at the right-hand of two gateways. Follow the bridleway signposted "Letchmore Heath ½ mile". At the end of the bridleway turn left into Grange Lane.

9. Take the right fork into the village (7.5 miles).

This is a picturesque village with a green, a pond and timber framed cottages dating from the 16th and 17th centuries. As well as a war memorial the village honoured its dead of the First World War by placing plaques on the houses of those who lost their lives, many with the words "Lest We Forget" and giving the name of the soldier who left that house never to return. The International Society for Krishna Consciousness occupies the former Piggotts Manor.

Cross the green by the war memorial and turn left into Back Lane, then turn right into Common Lane. Just before reaching the overhead power cables leave the lane along a gravel track to the right. Go through an open gate marked "The Cottage" (this is a public right of way) and then through a gap to the left of double iron gates. Follow the gravel track to its end between a house on the left and a whitewashed building on the right. Go through a double wooden gate and proceed straight on along the track and across a small metalled lane. Continue in the same direction along the gravel track with a field on the right and stables on the left.

10. The path narrows past a small bungalow on the left. Pass through a wooden kissing gate, turn sharp left and then sharp right onto a path between rows of trees. Pass through a metal kissing gate and go along the left hand edge of a large field. Carry on in the same direction to a broad track which joins from the left and continue right along this track. Where the track passes a small wood on the left hand side, turn right (south) onto the footpath which crosses a large field.

11. At the far side of the field turn left beside a large oak tree. Ignore the path on the right (35 yards beyond the oak tree) and keep to the field edge for another 85 yards. Go through the wooden gate in the hedge just past another large oak tree; this takes you into a wooded area. The footpath (right-of-way) goes directly ahead through the trees but an alternative is to turn right and proceed along a stone path with a fence on the right. This stone path curves round in an arc and where it rejoins the right-of-way walk due east about 15 yards across the grass to a wooden gate in the hedge. Go through the gate and continue through the middle of the long narrow field with the brick buildings of Little Kendals Farm on the left. As the field widens, keep to the middle of the field aiming towards a hedge and gate in the distance. Cross a concrete footbridge and head to a metal kissing gate in the hedge.

12. Go through this gate into Watling Street (9.2 miles).
Watling Street was the longest of the Roman roads in Britain, running from Dover, through London to Chester. Much of the original Roman road, including this section through southern Hertfordshire, is still a major highway.
Cross Watling Street, turn right for 100 yards and then turn left along a metalled road signposted to Hertsmere and Kendal Hall Farm. Where the road turns left keep straight on for 50 yards to reach a wooden gate at the right hand side of the farm lane. Go through this gate. Keeping the line of the pylons and power cables to your right, cross towards the bottom left hand corner of the field. Go through the wooden gate and continue into the next field for about 50 yards before turning right and crossing the wooden bridge. Turn left onto a footpath with scrub on both sides. Emerge at a rutted farm track. Turn left along the track with the railway line on your right. Where the track turns left away from the railway, you turn right and go under the railway arch (often flooded after storms). Continue on a track, crossing a footbridge at the ford in the stream. Turn right through the hedge, then left along the field with a hedge on the left, until reaching a road.

13. Cross the road with care as this is a blind corner with fast-moving traffic. Walk straight ahead (northeast) along a signposted footpath. Continue between two wooden fences for about 250 yards across a wooden footbridge and through a wooden gate. Continue along the edge of a large field with a fence on the right and trees and hedgerow on the left. At the end of the field go left through a gap and continue crossing a footbridge over a small stream then onto a path between hedges. Follow this path until it meets a farm track. Turn right onto this track and then bear left at the fork, keeping a horse gallop on your right,

and walk towards metal gates. Turn left through woodland and follow the path. Continue on the path past a metal gate on the left and another on the right. You then turn sharp left at another metal gate; do not go through the wooden kissing gate. Follow the path as it turns sharp right at yet another metal gate and continue up the hill until you reach a road (Woodhall Lane) (11.2 miles).

14. Turn right along this road and continue for a quarter-mile, passing Kitwells Lodge on your right until you reach a wooden gateway for Woodhall Spinney. Turn left and follow the path down to the road (Radlett Lane). Cross this lane and enter Shenley Park, turn left and shortly cross another footbridge to reach a gravel path. At this point turn left to reach the tearoom, car park and the start of the next leg (12.3 miles). Alternatively turn right to reach the village centre by following the main path until it reaches the lane. Cross and follow another path to reach the road and bus stop opposite the Black Lion pub (at the time of writing closed and threatened with demolition).

Shenley is an ancient settlement. Near the War Memorial stands an 18th-century lock-up. Porters Park, dating from the 13th century, was a large estate on the north-west edge of Shenley. This was the home of the architect, Nicholas Hawksmoor (d. 1736), who was Wren's assistant on St. Pauls. Admiral Lord Howe also lived there. He was First Lord of the Admiralty when Nelson was in his twenties and was made Admiral of the Fleet in 1796. A mental hospital, opened by King George V and Queen Mary in 1934, occupied part of the estate until 1996. The hospital water tower remains as a prominent landmark. Shenley Park has been created as part of the redevelopment of Shenley Hospital; excellent leaflets are available from the park office just off Radlett Lane. Further information about the Shenley Park Trust may be obtained from the Director on 01923 852629.

Leg 9 Shenley to Cuffley

Length 11.5 miles.
Start Radlett Lane, Shenley, WD7 9DW, TL182006. Free car parking.
Finish Cuffley Station, EN6 4H, TL 307028. Pay car parking.
Maps Explorer 182, 174, Landranger 166.
Public Transport Shenley (see Leg 8). Cuffley has mainline trains and local buses.
Pubs/Refreshments Shenley (Café and toilets); Blackhorse Lane, South Mimms; Heath Road, Potters Bar; Northaw; Cuffley.

The Route

On this walk we cross trunk road and railway routes radiating from London - M25, A1(M), the old Great North Road at Potters Bar and two railway routes from Kings Cross/Moorgate. But it is surprising how rural this walk is and the variety of scenery to be experienced.

The Walk

1. Start at Shenley Park Car Park off Radlett Lane. Turn right at Car Park Exit (left leads out to Radlett Lane). Walk past the Walled Garden on your left. Go right at "Stable Flats". Turn diagonally left at waymark post and then follow the red Shenley Circular Walk 1 waymarks. At the wooden double gate turn left. *You are now following the boundary of the Porter Housing Estate, with the hedge on your left, giving views of the Cricket Ground laid out by W. G. Grace and, roughly diagonally right and on a clear day, there are fine views across the vale of St Albans. Note the M25, the previous Pastoral Centre, and the distinctive tower of Napsbury Hospital, and St Albans cathedral on the skyline.* Following the well defined path, bear left down the incline, then right at red Footpath 1 sign, then through woodland, turning left at the T-junction, and right at bottom of slope. Turn left when you reach the road (Porters Park Drive). At the mini-roundabout cross the road (Black Lion Hill). Join on your immediate left the grass track that runs parallel to the road (this is the B5378 in the direction of St Albans).

2. You soon have a bank on your left down to the road. At the waymark post follow the cross field path on your right to a patch of woodland which you go through towards some pylons and cross another field bearing slightly right to a farm track.

3. At the waymark post at the farm track turn right for 10 yards or so, then go through a gap in the hedge on your left. This leads to another crossfield path. Bear slightly right and make for the middle of the copse

you see in front of you. At the next stile bear half right towards the right hand edge of the copse, walk past the abandoned brick building and, ignoring the farm track, bear slightly left and make for a stile in the hedgerow ahead of you. Walk to the left of the stand of trees, and join another footpath leading to a stile back onto the farm track. Turn left and follow the track up to a stile on your left opposite the barn (Shenley Stud Farm). Cross the stile and corner of a field taking you to a stile on to Rectory Lane.

4. Ignore the stile and signpost in front of you. Turn left along Rectory Lane for 250 yards as far as "Grassfields" on your left. Go through the kissing gate opposite (post and sign) and make for the kissing gate at the bottom left hand corner of the field. Follow a fence on your left to a kissing gate into a narrow tarred lane (Dovers Green). Cross the lane and carry on through the kissing gate opposite. Walk straight across an open field following the overhead lines to a kissing gate at the far left corner. Follow the hedge on your left in the next field and two kissing gates bring you to Packhorse Lane alongside Rabley Park Farm.

5. Cross the road and go through the kissing gate opposite, near the post and sign "Public Footpath to S.Mimms ¾ mile". Cross an open field bearing right to a kissing gate. Go through the kissing gate (notice the plaque on the gate as it was provided by The Friends of The Hertfordshire Way) into a field, and descend to a bridge by a stream (Catharine Bourne).

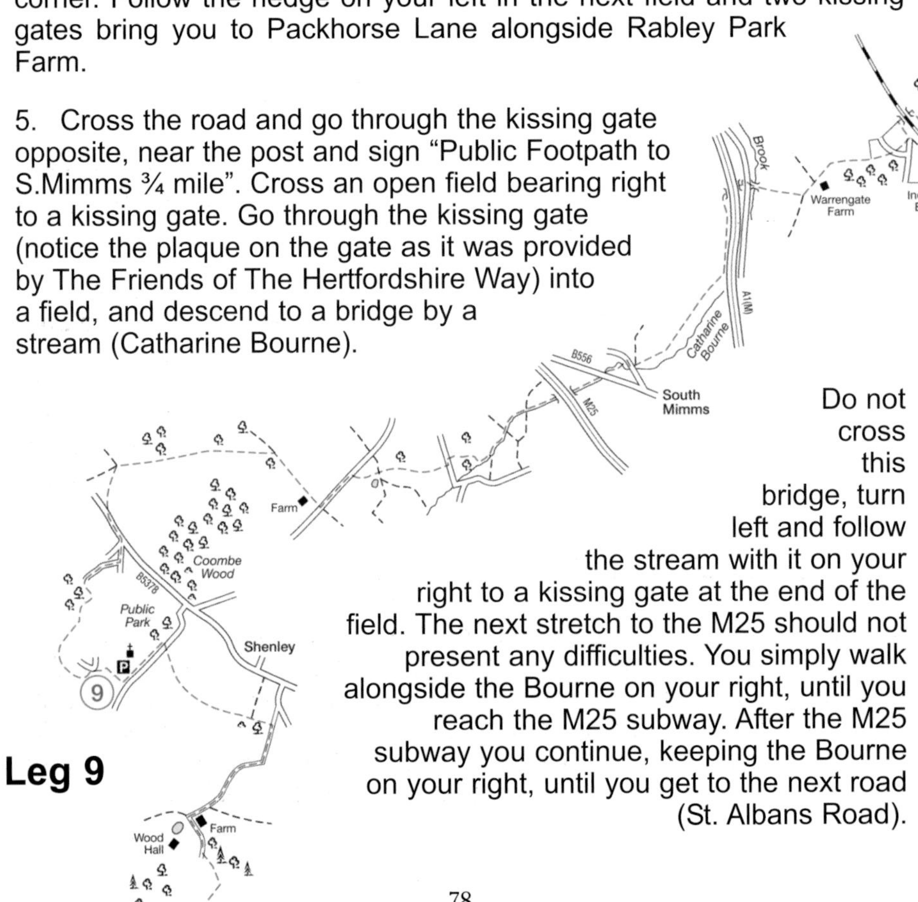

Do not cross this bridge, turn left and follow the stream with it on your right to a kissing gate at the end of the field. The next stretch to the M25 should not present any difficulties. You simply walk alongside the Bourne on your right, until you reach the M25 subway. After the M25 subway you continue, keeping the Bourne on your right, until you get to the next road (St. Albans Road).

6. Cross over to the signpost (almost opposite) and follow the Bourne again but keeping it now on your left for the next short stretch. Cross the bridge and then walk between two gardens and houses to join Blackhorse Lane (3.9 miles).

The Black Horse pub is across the road on your left.

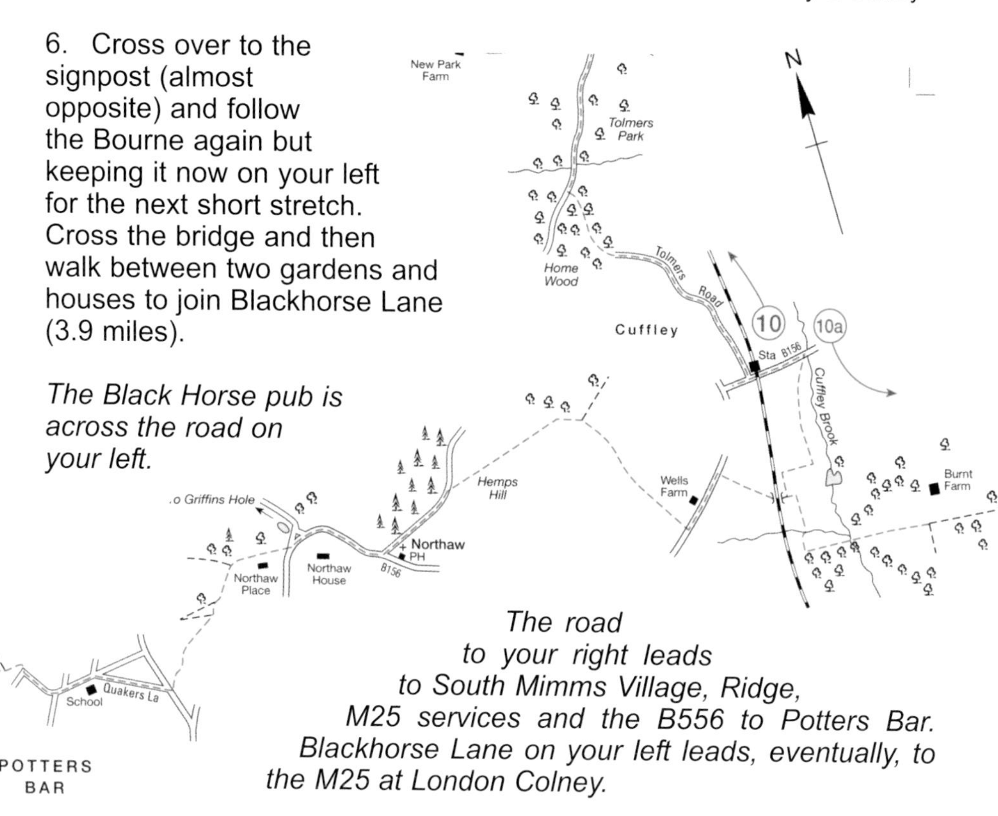

The road to your right leads to South Mimms Village, Ridge, M25 services and the B556 to Potters Bar. Blackhorse Lane on your left leads, eventually, to the M25 at London Colney.

7. Cross the road, walk 25 yards to your right and on your left you will see a tarred lane between houses with a signpost at the end by a kissing gate. Go through the gate and follow the hedge on your right via another kissing gate and make for a wooden pylon where you turn left onto a wide fenced track. Make for the A1(M) on this track. When you get to the A1(M) boundary you follow it until you get to the road subway. Go through the subway and proceed to and cross the old A1 and enter the field opposite.

8. Use the footbridge in front of you to cross the ford of Mimmshall Brook. Go straight ahead with the stream on your left until you reach Warrengate Farm. Cross the brook on a substantial farm bridge and turn immediately right. Keep this brook on your right until you reach the Cranbourne Industrial Estate road. Cross the road to the signpost opposite and follow a short stretch of path by the brook to bring you to another road. Turn left and walk for approximately 50 yards to a subway under the railway. This brings you to the Potters Bar Golf Course.

Nelson's Column

9. Turn right after the kissing gate, on to the golf course keeping the railway embankment on your immediate right. When you come to a large diameter pipe go under it noting the pillbox on your right. You should now see a series of waymarks with a ditch on your right. You pass a number of footbridges, with a turn to the left after the second bridge. Shortly after you pass another pillbox on your left watch out for the waymark that points right over a grassed bridge (a brick built drainage channel). Cross at this point and you enter a path leading up the slope through the trees. You come out into a very short drive with gates to your left, turn right here and then left on to Mountway (6.9 miles).

Potters Bar. *First recorded in 1387, refers to a former gate between estates along the Great North Road. It owes its development from a small hamlet, initially, to the Great North Road and later, from 1850, to the railway from London, which turned it into a commuter town. In the 2011 census it had a population of just under 23,000.*

WWII pill box on Potters Bar golf course

10. Proceed down Mountway to the junction of Darkes Lane and Church Road. *(If you wish to go to Potters Bar for the railway and bus stations, shops etc turn right here into Darkes Lane and continue for 800 yards but return here to continue the route).* Turn left into Church Road and look out for Quakers Lane on your right. On entering Church Road, turning immediately left again into Heath Road will bring you to the Builder's Arms pub. Turn left on leaving the pub, and right again into Osborne Road to bring you back to Church Road opposite Quakers Lane. Follow Quakers Lane to its junction with Hatfield Road and look for a kissing gate opposite.

Between Northaw and Cuffley Brook

11. Turn left and following the hedgerow, ignoring a kissing gate on your left, go through the opening in the hedge over a board walk, then carry on diagonally right across the open field and at the corner follow the hedge line on your right along a well defined path. At the kissing gate follow the path at the right edge of a small stretch of woodland until you get to an open field.

Northaw House and some new properties will be diagonally right of you. Follow a well defined path and, at the bottom left of the field, cross a footbridge and then bear right. With the gardens immediately on your right you come out on to Coopers Lane at St Just.

Northaw is a Conservation area. It has a long history linked with the Abbot and monks of St. Albans Abbey certainly from about 800 AD to 1539 when the Abbey lands were dissolved. The church is Victorian; the old one was burnt down in 1881. The attraction of Northaw Common was initially as a hunting area with Enfield Chase also on its borders. Northaw became popular with the gentry and a number of fine houses survive. On this route you pass Northaw Place, now a residential development, and Northaw House. If you have an interest in industrial archaeology and wish to know a little about what was the main source of pure water for over two centuries for the inhabitants of Northaw, turn left along Well Road. After about half a mile, near the boundary post, on your right, you will see a public footpath sign pointing into the wood (Well Wood). 150 yards or so in, you will see Griffins Hole Spring which has been cleaned out and restored in 2003–4. The 1806 Enclosure Act and the 1895 Survey of the Local Footpaths by the newly established Parish Council both refer to "the right of carriage way for the parishioners of Northaw" to collect their own water or have it collected by water cart from Griffins Hole or, as later happened, have it pumped to the (eventually) four tanks – total capacity 84,000 gallons – under the village green next to the church. If you decide to investigate this site allow about 45 minutes extra time.

12. At the junction of Well Road, Coopers Lane and Judges Hill cross over and turn left along Judges Hill, and up to Northaw Village Green, War Memorial, Church (8.4 miles) and two pubs. Go left at the Sun Pub down Vineyards Road for about 650 yards to a kissing gate on the right just beyond Carramore House, pointing to Cuffley. Follow the path down to the valley through kissing gates gradually dropping to the valley bottom. Cross a footbridge and turn right following the Cuffley Brook on your right. At a junction of two paths carry straight on along the farm track for 0.8 miles to Northaw Road East.

Along this stretch you pass the Pumping Station on your left. The Kings Well was a chalybeate spring (iron salts rich), popular with James I and Charles II and the gentry. Charles had a large marquee erected there for their accommodation. It was still famous enough in 1809 to get a special mention in John Cary's Map of Hertfordshire. The name still survives in Cuffley street names like Kingswell Drive. The site of The King's Well is not precisely known but was in the area of the Pumping Station.

13. Go left along the road for about 250 yards passing playing fields on your right to a signpost at the head of a track. Turn right and follow the track under the railway bridge.

14. Immediately after the railway bridge turn left at the waymarks. Follow the hedge parallel to the railway, then at right angles along the field edge and left through an opening. Follow the line of the hedge on your left, through two kissing gates, and then bear diagonally right over a wooden bridge and continue diagonally right across the small field to join Cuffley Hill. Turn left to the village and railway station car park (11.5 miles).

Evidence of prehistoric settlement at Cuffley and some Roman activity has been discovered in the area. It gained national fame in September 1916 when the first German military airship destroyed in this country was shot down near the Plough pub in Cuffley by the night fighter pilot William Leefe Robinson VC whose memorial is on East Ridgeway near the pub and whose name survives as a Cuffley street name. Cuffley, with the arrival of the railway in 1910, began to develop as a commuter village and particularly in the last sixty years has rapidly expanded with quite a range of shops in the village centre.

At this point you have a choice of following the original route into Hertford (Leg 10) or taking a two leg route to Hertford by Broxbourne Woods and the River Lee (Legs 10A and 10B). The directions for these alternative legs follow after Leg 10.

Leg 10 Cuffley to Hertford

Length 12.6 miles.
Start Cuffley Station, EN6 4HY, TL 307028. Pay car parking.
Finish Parliament Square, Hertford, SG14 1EX, TL 326125. Town car parks (pay)
Maps Explorer 182, 174, Landranger 166.
Public Transport Cuffley (see Leg 9). Hertford has two main line stations with different routes and a bus station.
Pubs/Refreshments several on route.

The Route

Starting from Cuffley, the route goes somewhat west of north through Newgate Street to West End. From there it proceeds in an easterly direction through Essendon and Little Berkhamsted to Bayford. It finally goes in a northerly direction to Hertford. The route takes us through several pretty villages. Northaw Great Wood, just off the start of this leg, with its three marked circular paths, is very popular with local people as a leisure resource for walking and relaxation.

The Walk

1. On leaving Cuffley Station turn right and in 80 yards turn right again along Tolmers Road. Follow this to its end (about 1 mile) and continue along a footpath running uphill into a wood with a fence on the right. On reaching a road, turn right and follow the road uphill for about half a mile to Newgate Street. (***This road is very busy and has no pavement so do take care.*** *A claim, by the late Hywel Morris on behalf of the Ramblers' Association, for a right of way on the opposite side of the road was the subject of a public enquiry in 2011. The Inspector ruled that the evidence was not sufficient and he declined to confirm the order*). Turn left at the roundabout and in 50 yards take the left fork, New Park Road (1.7 miles).

Essendon Country Club

2. Follow this to the end of the houses and continue straight on along a track. In about half a mile follow the track round a corner to the right and then continue straight on and emerge between houses on to a road. Turn left along the road and in 30 yards take the right fork (Cucumber Lane). After half a mile take the bridleway on the left and follow it along the inside edge of the wood. Continue through trees and bushes before emerging at Warren Wood Manor. Follow the Manor drive to reach a road, passing several houses on the left en route.

3. Go straight across on to a public footpath and then turn right in 150 yards at buildings. Keep going down hill to emerge into the open. Keep straight ahead on a path through low scrub and then between hedges. At a waymark post turn left and follow a path with a stream to its right. Cross a wooden bridge and bear left by a waymark post. Follow the path uphill with a hedge on the right.

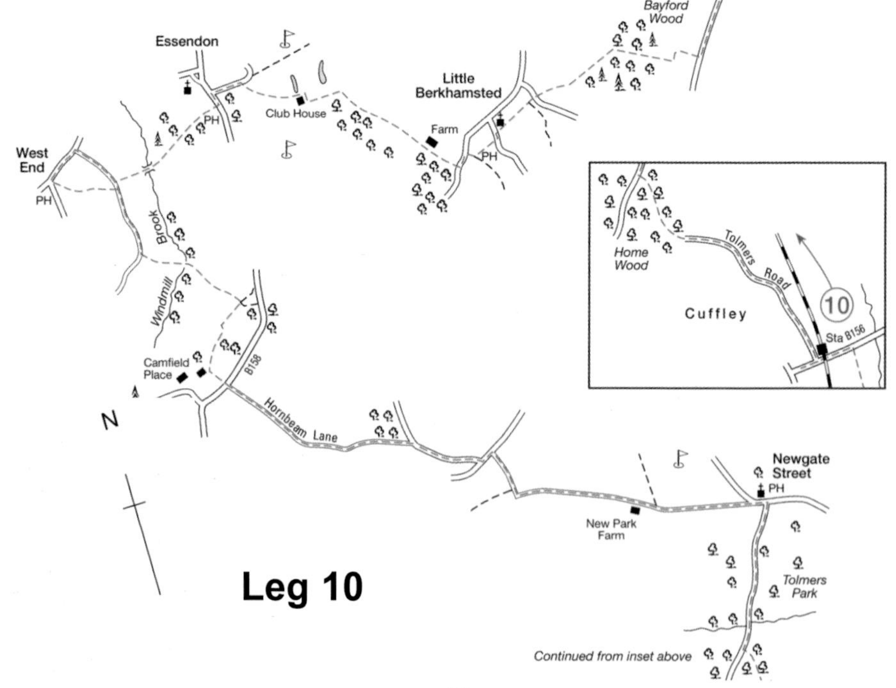

Winter scene near New Park Farm, Newgate Street

Go through a kissing gate and turn right along a track. After about 800 yards, turn left at a waymark post and follow a footpath through a kissing gate and then along the edge of a field with the hedge on the right. Cross a stile and reach a road at West End by The Candlestick pub (5.5 miles).

4. Turn right along the road and in a quarter of a mile take the byway to the right. After half a mile, take the path to the left. Proceed downhill with the hedge on the left, cross a bridge, bear diagonally left, and take the footpath uphill through the wood. Emerge by the pavilion of Essendon Cricket Club and follow the edge of a field, with a wall on the right, to a road (6.5 miles).
Essendon has the Rose & Crown and the former Salisbury Crest inn (now a private dwelling) which dates from the 17th century, and a church which has several monumental brasses. Look for a stone on the outside commemorating repairs after a Zeppelin raid in the First World War.
Turn left, then in 50 yards turn right along School Lane. Pass the village hall on the left and in 40 yards take the footpath to the right (signposted Little Berkhamsted 1¼ miles). Follow the path into Essendon Country Club, pass in front of the clubhouse, and follow the waymarked path to reach white buildings at the bottom of the hill.

5. Go between the buildings and take the path going diagonally right uphill behind the cottage and follow it past farm buildings to emerge on a road. Turn left and in 100 yards turn right onto a bridleway. In 50 yards go through a kissing gate on the left into Little Berkhamsted Cricket Club ground and follow the left hand edge of the ground to the road (7.9 miles).
Little Berkhamsted has the Five Horseshoes. Look out, while in this area, for the noted landmark Stratton's Folly built in 1789, a folly in the form of a five storey tower built by retired Admiral John Stratton, which can be seen from miles around.
Turn left along the road and in 50 yards turn right (just before the churchyard) and pass through a kissing gate onto a public footpath. Follow this through a further two gates to a road.

6. Turn right and in 15 yards turn left to cross a stile on to a footpath (signposted Bayford 1 mile). After two further stiles the path bears diagonally left across two fields, passing the corner of a wood. Continue over a bridge into a wood. In about 200 yards the path turns right and then left at the waymarks. Continue uphill across a track and shortly cross a stile into a field. Follow the field edge, with the hedge on the left,

Stratton's Folly, Little Berkhamsted

and cross a stile at the field corner onto a path, which quickly becomes a track, and follow this to Ashendene Road.

7. Turn left along the road and proceed into Bayford (9.3 miles).
The church of St Mary at Bayford dates only from 1870 but it is built on the site of two early churches and contains relics from them including a 15th-century font. There are some very pretty cottages around the pond.
Pass the Baker Arms on the right and continue straight on along Bayford Green. The road bends right and then left between buildings and continues as a track between trees. In 100 yards take the footpath on the right through a kissing gate. At the end of the field go through a kissing gate on the right and go down the next field with a wire fence on the left. Enter a small wood and go through a kissing gate on the left into a long field.

8. Follow the edge of this field with a wire fence and a railway line on the right for about 0.8 miles. About 100 yards from the end of the field, the path crosses a wooden footbridge on the right and continues in the same direction through woods with the railway on the right for a further mile. After a short section between wire-mesh fences on both sides turn right and cross the railway track by a footbridge. Follow the path to the left across two fields to a road.

9. Turn left at the road and then right up Mandeville Road. Follow this for about 800 yards, turn right into Wilton Crescent, and in 20 yards right again into a footpath. Pass a school on the left and at the end of the path cross the road into Queens Road. Just past the junction with Highfield Road turn right through barriers and follow the path down. At the bottom of the hill turn left and continue with the stream on the right. Reach and continue along a road and at the T-junction cross straight over and take the footpath through the churchyard. Swing left round the church, and leave by the main gate. Take the underpass on the right, walk down Church Street to the Shire Hall

Information on Hertford is given in the introduction to Leg 11. To go to Hertford East railway station and the bus station, go along the right hand side of the Shire Hall, cross the Square to the far right corner and proceed along Railway Street. The bus station is along the first road to the left. For the railway station, continue along the road and go left at the roundabout. The station is a further 200 yards on the left. For Hertford North station, go to the right out of Parliament Square and follow this road (The Wash, then St Andrew Street, then North Road) for about 0.8 miles.

Leg 10A Cuffley to Broxbourne

Length 12 miles.
Start Cuffley Station, EN6 4HY, TL 307028. Station car park (pay).
Finish Broxbourne Station, EN10 7AW, TL 373072. Station car park (pay)
Maps Explorer 174, Landranger 166.
Public Transport Train, local buses.
Pubs/Refreshments Goff's Oak, Wormley West End.

The Route

This walk takes you through a large area of ancient woodland, including the county's only National Nature Reserve. Broxbourne Woods NNR is made up of four individual woods: Broxbourne, Bencroft, Wormley and Hoddesdonpark Woods.

The Walk

1. Turn left outside the approach road to Cuffley station into Station Road. Walk for 350 yards down Station Road. Cross the road with care and take the footpath on the right opposite the entrance to Brook Farm through a kissing gate. Cross the field diagonally to the far right hand corner. Cross the stream at a footbridge and follow the path to a kissing gate. Continue beside a fence, cross over a ditch and through another kissing gate, then continue along the right-hand edge of the next field. Go through another kissing gate and immediately turn right to follow the right-hand edge of a field, turning left at the end to go alongside the railway embankment. On reaching a track, which runs beneath the railway arch, turn left away from the railway and then follow the track as it swings around to the right. With the railway viaduct on your right, follow the track as it swings left and away from the railway. Stay on this track for another 800 yards, over a stream and uphill, then turn left along another broad track. Continue on this track past Burnt Farm on the right-hand side, after which the track becomes a metalled lane. As you reach higher ground, note the extensive views across the valley to Cuffley on your left-hand side. Some 800 yards beyond the farm there is a double gate across the lane. Go through a gap to the left of this gate and in a few yards turn right into Silver Street.

2. Turn left at the sign to Poyndon Farm. As the drive swings right, go through a kissing gate and continue straight ahead. Go down the right-hand edge of the field and through another kissing gate into a path between a hedge on the right and a fence on the left. The path continues between a barbed-wire fence on the right and gardens on the

Leg 10A

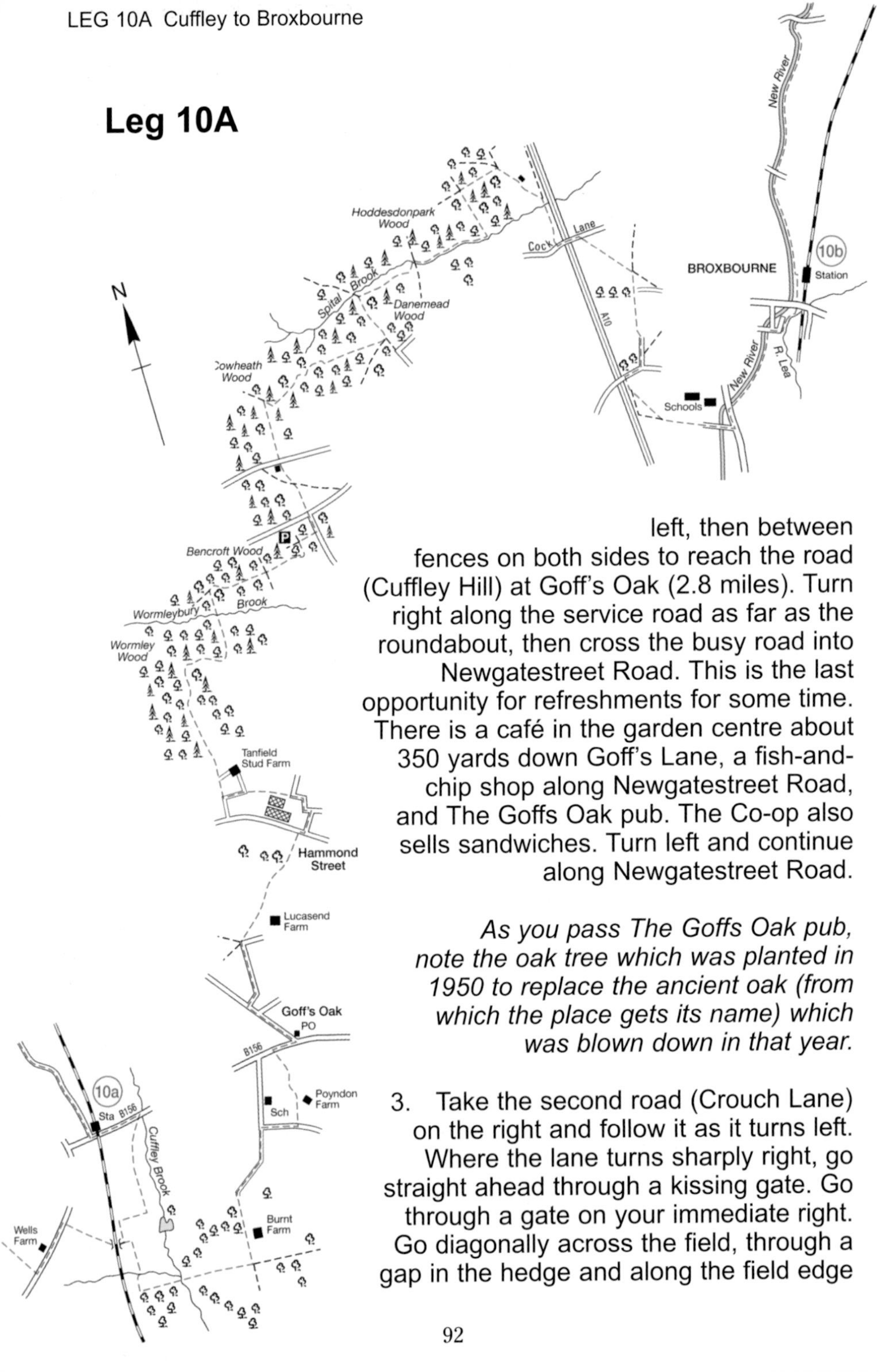

left, then between fences on both sides to reach the road (Cuffley Hill) at Goff's Oak (2.8 miles). Turn right along the service road as far as the roundabout, then cross the busy road into Newgatestreet Road. This is the last opportunity for refreshments for some time. There is a café in the garden centre about 350 yards down Goff's Lane, a fish-and-chip shop along Newgatestreet Road, and The Goffs Oak pub. The Co-op also sells sandwiches. Turn left and continue along Newgatestreet Road.

As you pass The Goffs Oak pub, note the oak tree which was planted in 1950 to replace the ancient oak (from which the place gets its name) which was blown down in that year.

3. Take the second road (Crouch Lane) on the right and follow it as it turns left. Where the lane turns sharply right, go straight ahead through a kissing gate. Go through a gate on your immediate right. Go diagonally across the field, through a gap in the hedge and along the field edge

with scrub on your right. Leave the field at its right hand corner and cross the ditch. Go right up steps into a field and cross the field diagonally. Cross a stile and keep on in the same direction to a kissing gate which leads into a path between bushes, with a fence on the right and a small wooded area on the left. Follow the path to reach a kissing gate and emerge at the road in Hammond Street.

Cuffley viaduct

4. Cross the road, turn right and then take the first turning left into Smith's Lane. At the T-junction turn left again into Bread and Cheese Lane. The lane turns right and then left, and where it turns right again, carry on straight ahead along a wide grassy footpath. Where the path joins a tarmac track continue in the same direction, and where this turns left, take the right turn along an unsurfaced track (marked Tanfield Yard Private Road). After 100 yards, where the main track reaches the gates of the yard, continue straight ahead towards a pylon on a green lane between hedges (4.6 miles).

5. Turn left alongside the stream for 20 yards, then cross the stream and enter woods at a stile. Turn right along a path which climbs through the edge of the wood.

Coal Post in Wormley Wood

The next 4 miles or so of the walk will take you through three of the four woods which make up Broxbourne Woods NNR, an SSSI consisting mainly of hornbeam and sessile oak. There is little doubt that Wormley Wood has been a woodland site since the end of the last Ice Age. It was first mentioned in documents in the 6th century, in association with Ermine Street.

Your route follows clearly established footpaths and bridleways, and although many sections do not appear as public rights-of-way on the OS map you will find that most of them have been well waymarked by the County Council or Broxbourne Council. After 350 yards the path joins a bridleway. Continue in the same direction along the bridleway and follow it for 700 yards as it meanders through the woods, across higher ground and past a coal post before descending to a stream (Wormleybury Brook). Cross the stream at the footbridge and continue up the slope for 200 yards to reach the National Nature Reserve notice board between Wormley Wood and Bencroft Wood.

6. Bear right through the fence into Bencroft Wood and after about 40 yards turn sharp right off the bridleway onto a footpath. Follow this path for 700 yards, maintaining the same direction, through woodland with views across open fields to the right in some places. Notice the ancient ditch and bank with coppiced hornbeams. The path undulates, crossing two small gullies via steps and plank bridges. Ignore crossing paths. At the end of a section of boardwalk, the path turns 90° left and in 100 yards emerges through a gap in a fence to reach a bridleway. Turn right onto the bridleway and continue until it reaches a minor road at Emanuel Pollards (6.1 miles).

To reach the Woodman & Olive pub / restaurant, turn right down the road and follow it round the bend to the left.

7. Turn left up the minor road to the T-junction at White Stubbs Lane. Although this is a country lane it is notorious for speeding traffic, **so cross with care.** Go through the kissing gate ahead and continue in the same direction across the fields through two kissing gates. Take the footpath straight ahead towards Pembridge Farm, go through a kissing gate and then two gates between the farm house and the barn to reach Pembridge Lane. Cross the lane and go through a sequence of three kissing gates into a field. Go diagonally across this field to reach a kissing gate in the dip at the far right-hand corner. Cross the stream (Spital Brook) by the footbridge and follow the path half-right up the slope on the opposite side and through a gap in the fence. Go ahead for 200 yards and where this path joins another path at a T-junction turn sharp right. Follow the path downhill for about 50 yards to a waymark

post which shows the definitive right-of-way going to your left. Although this path has been badly damaged by heavy machinery you should follow the waymark posts for about 350 yards to meet another path at right-angles. Turn right and follow this path downhill for about 50 yards to reach a stream; cross by the footbridge.

8. Turn left along the path, go through a kissing gate to enter a conifer plantation and in about 100 yards turn right on the waymarked path through the trees. This path continues in the same direction up a gentle slope for 120 yards and then swings left through a kissing gate at the edge of the plantation. Go through and follow the path across Broxbourne Common, an area of mixed woodland, to reach a bridleway. Turn left then left again at the edge of the common onto a wide bridleway. Go past a thatched house with outbuildings and follow the bridleway downhill. At the bottom of the slope turn right through a kissing gate into Danemead Nature Reserve and follow the path with the stream on your left for 500 yards. Leave the nature reserve by crossing two footbridges at right angles to each other and cross the bridleway (Ermine Street, 8 miles).

Ermine Street was the Roman road which ran from London toYork. The name is derived from a Saxon personal name. The road was used long after the Romans left; it gradually fell into disuse but was still used as a drove road until the 19th century.

In Hoddesdonpark Wood is a moated site, probably 13th century, which is a scheduled ancient monument. A document of 1290 details the restocking of Hoddesdonpark Wood with two bucks and two does from the Forest of Essex. The moated site is thought to be the location of the park-keeper's lodge. Nothing remains of the buildings.

9. Go through a kissing gate into Hoddesdonpark Wood. Turn right alongside the fence and follow the path as it turns left and runs beside the stream. After about 500 yards note the moated site (a slight mound surrounded by a sedge-filled ditch) to the left of the path, then turn left up the slope on a straight, wide track with ditches on both sides. Ignoring the footpath with a wooden footbridge on the right-hand side, continue uphill for 350 yards to reach a broad crossing path. Turn right and follow the path to a kissing gate. Leave the wood and turn right onto the track towards Hoddesdon Lodge. Pass between the house and outbuildings and go through a kissing gate into the field. Walk down the slope towards the left-hand edge of the field, aiming towards the pylon. Go through a kissing gate and continue in the same direction down to the corner of the next field, leaving by a kissing gate to reach a footpath by the embankment to the A10 dual carriageway.

Wood anemones, Hoddesdonpark Wood

10. Turn right along this footpath, staying on the western side of the A10, to reach Cock Lane (9.2 miles). Turn left along the lane, cross the bridge over the A10, and after another 50 yards turn right through a kissing gate onto a footpath. Follow the footpath beside a line of trees with houses on the left. Go through a kissing gate. Continue in the same direction and in 50 yards go through another kissing gate between houses on the left and trees on the right. Go through two more kissing gates to reach a junction of paths.
If you wish to cut short the walk at this point, continue in the same direction along a footpath between wooden fences, then follow Park Lane as far as the main road (A1170), cross at the traffic lights and continue down Station Road to Broxbourne Station.

11. Bear right along the bridleway with a wooden fence and houses to your left for 500 yards, eventually emerging into Allard Way. At the end of Allard Way turn right into Baas Hill, then left at the footpath sign (actually a restricted byway) just before the road bridge over the A10. Go through the kissing gate into Top Field & Cozens Grove Nature Reserve, then diagonally across the field towards trees. Within the trees cross a footbridge then turn left downhill, passing between tennis courts on the right and the playing fields of Broxbourne School on the left.

(*Please note that at the time of publication of this guidebook there are proposals to relocate Broxbourne School into new premises to be built adjacent to the Hertfordshire Way. This will probably lead to an application to divert this public right-of-way. We are unable to predict when this might be or what route any possible diversion might take*).
Continue into Cozens Lane West, which crosses the New River (10.8 miles). Turn left along the main road (A1170) and cross at the pedestrian crossing. Pass through a kissing gate and follow the New River path (along the right-hand bank) for 700 yards, then turn right down Mill Lane just before reaching Broxbourne Church.

New River at Broxbourne

The New River was constructed between 1608 and 1613 to bring drinking water from Chadwell and Amwell Springs to London. It was built along the 100 foot contour and was then about 40 miles long. On the next leg of the walk you will meet the New River again.

Broxbourne Church is predominantly 15th century, with a 16th century north chapel built by Sir William Say.

There was a mill at Broxbourne in the Domesday survey. The remains standing now are of a 19th century mill that burnt down in 1949 when it was being used as an engineering workshop. Corn was last ground there in the 1890s.

12. At the foot of Mill Lane turn left past the ruins of the mill, through the car park and along the footpath between the mill stream and the railway. Just before reaching the railway cross the stream by the footbridge on the left and continue through the station car park to reach Broxbourne Station (12.0 miles).

Leg 10B Broxbourne to Hertford

Length 12.5 miles.
Start Broxbourne Station, EN10 7AW, TL 373072. Station car park (pay)
Finish Parliament Square, Hertford, SG14 1EX, TL 326125. Town car parks (pay).
Maps Explorer 174, Landranger 166.
Public Transport Train, numerous buses linking towns.
Pubs/Refreshments Rye House, Stanstead Abbotts, Great Amwell, Ware, Hertford.

The Route

This walk, which follows the Lea valley along the New River and the Lee Navigation with a diversion to the Ash valley, twice crosses the Greenwich meridian. The route can be divided into smaller stages as it passes through all the intermediate stations on the railway line between Broxbourne and Hertford.

The Walk

1. Immediately outside Broxbourne Station climb the steps up the embankment to reach the New River Path. Turn right and follow the path for 1.2 miles to a pumping station at Essex Road. Cross this busy road with care and continue along the New River Path for a further 0.6 miles as far as the road at Rye House Station (1.9 miles). Turn right onto the road, cross the railway, and then turn left onto the River Lea towpath.

Across the river opposite the pub stands Rye House Gatehouse, all that remains of a fortified manor built in 1443 and a fine example of early brickwork. In 1683 it was the setting for the Rye House Plot (planned but not carried out) to assassinate Charles II and James, Duke of York. Later it became the central feature of an extensive Victorian pleasure park. Rye Meads Nature Reserve now extends along the opposite bank.

2. Follow the towpath for 1.2 miles as far as Stanstead Abbotts and turn right onto the High Street. At the roundabout at the eastern end of the High Street turn left into Cappell Lane.

The Clock House standing on the corner of Cappell Lane was originally a medieval chapel. From 1635 it housed a grammar school founded by Sir Edward Baesh. The school closed in 1879 and the building became known as the Clock House. St Andrew's Church was built in 1881 for Thomas Buxton of Easnye. It replaced St James' near Stanstead Bury as the parish church.

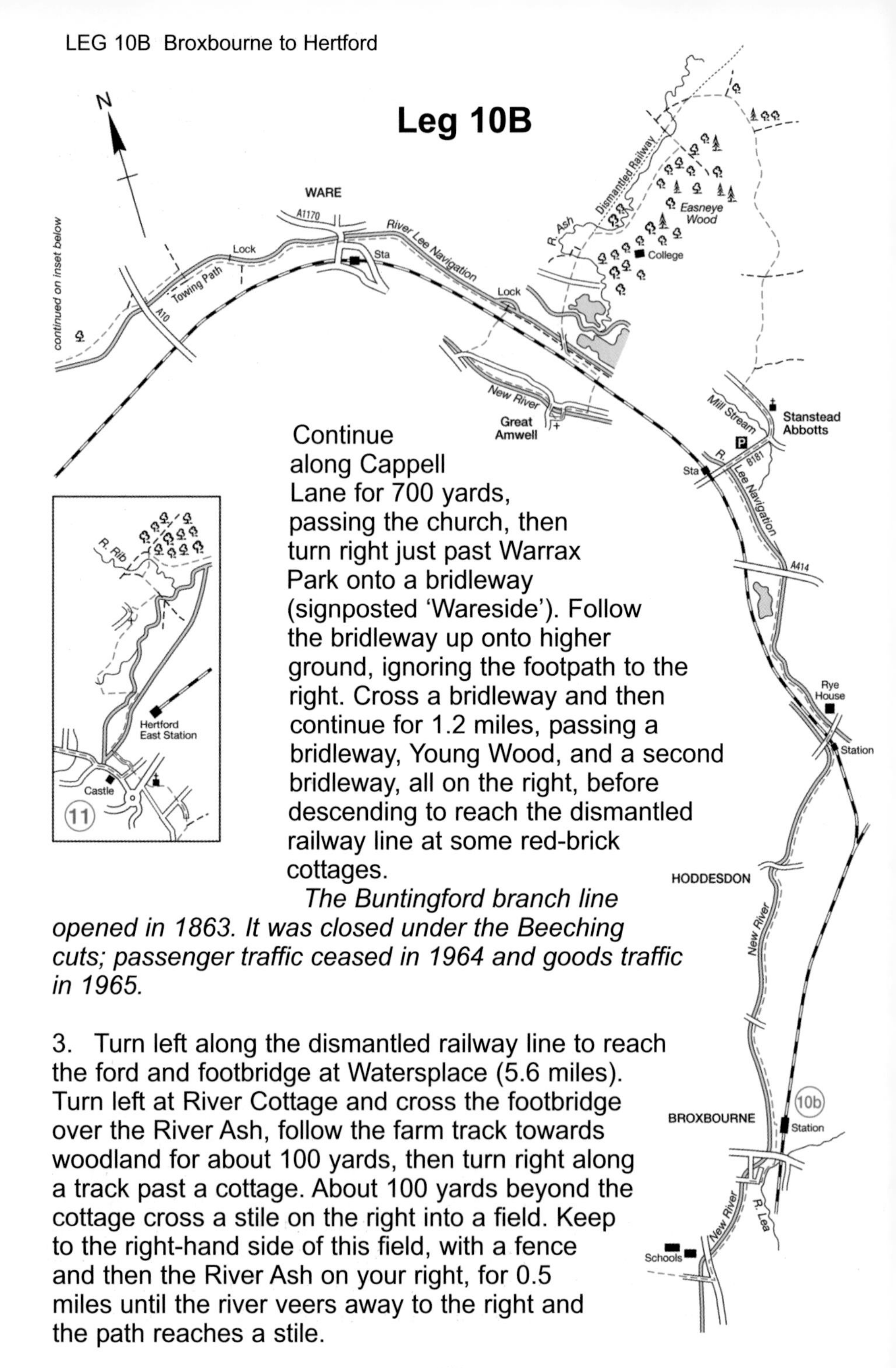

Continue along Cappell Lane for 700 yards, passing the church, then turn right just past Warrax Park onto a bridleway (signposted 'Wareside'). Follow the bridleway up onto higher ground, ignoring the footpath to the right. Cross a bridleway and then continue for 1.2 miles, passing a bridleway, Young Wood, and a second bridleway, all on the right, before descending to reach the dismantled railway line at some red-brick cottages.

The Buntingford branch line opened in 1863. It was closed under the Beeching cuts; passenger traffic ceased in 1964 and goods traffic in 1965.

3. Turn left along the dismantled railway line to reach the ford and footbridge at Watersplace (5.6 miles). Turn left at River Cottage and cross the footbridge over the River Ash, follow the farm track towards woodland for about 100 yards, then turn right along a track past a cottage. About 100 yards beyond the cottage cross a stile on the right into a field. Keep to the right-hand side of this field, with a fence and then the River Ash on your right, for 0.5 miles until the river veers away to the right and the path reaches a stile.

The public right of way cuts sharply uphill to the left and loops back down to the right to the disused railway line but most walkers cross the stile and follow the bed of the disused railway line to a wooden footbridge over the River Ash (note the remains of the brick piers of the old railway bridge on your right). Rejoin the railway bed, and follow it under the road bridge, through a kissing gate to enter Lee Valley Regional Park. Continue along Amwell Walkway over a wide footbridge with flooded gravel pits on either side.

Sand and gravel have been quarried in this area since 1973. Amwell Nature Reserve, owned by the Herts & Middlesex Wildlife Trust, is on the left. Development for wildlife conservation started in 1983 with the aim of encouraging as wide a variety of wildlife as possible. Otters were re-introduced in 1991.

Ash valley

4. On reaching the River Lee Navigation, cross by the footbridge, ignore steps on the right and continue along the disused railway line. After 150 yards, the path turns left. (One of the Lee Valley Park picnic areas is a few yards ahead on the river bank). Before reaching the river turn right onto a concrete path, then right again to reach the railway line. Cross with care and continue along the track to the road. Cross the road and ascend the steps opposite to return to the New River Path. Turn right along the path and in 100 yards turn left over the footbridge.

On the islands there is a monument to the builder of the New River, Sir Hugh Myddleton, and an ode to Emma's Well. The well is situated just to the east of the pool and is one of the springs which fed the New River. St John's Church is 11th century, much restored, with a 15th-century tower and is one of only three churches in Hertfordshire with a Norman apse (we pass one of the others later on this walk at Bengeo). In the churchyard is the tomb of the Mylne family, engineers and architects of the New River, the gravestone of Harold Abrahams (Olympic gold medallist in 1924) and a set of stocks.

Gazebos at Ware

5. Ascend the steps to the church (7.4 miles). Follow the path to the right around the church (note: the waymark is located beyond your turn) and leave the churchyard by the gate opposite the George IV pub. Turn right and immediately left down a steep footpath to the road bridge over the New River. Go left through the kissing gate onto the New River Path

and continue as far as the next road bridge. Leave the path by the kissing gate, turn right across the minor road and take the gravel track. Cross the railway line with care to reach the River Lea towpath at Hardmead Lock. Turn left onto the towpath and continue as far as Ware. Cross the main road and resume the towpath on the bank opposite the Saracen's Head pub (9.2 miles).

Along the opposite bank are some 18th century gazebos, all listed buildings. These are unique to Ware; although there are individual gazebos elsewhere in Britain, this is the only surviving group. Virtually every building in Water Row (the south side of Ware High Street) was an inn at some time during the period 1400 – 1700. Because of the heavy vehicles used in Ware's malting trade the roads were often impassable and this led to the setting up of England's first turnpike at Wadesmill in 1663. With the prospect of having to pay a toll, much of the traffic tried to find other routes, leading to a diminution of trade for the inns. To attract new business the inns laid out riverside gardens with summer houses or gazebos.

6. Continue along the towpath for 0.7 miles, past the GlaxoSmithKline site on the opposite bank, and immediately beyond the last of the factory buildings cross the river by means of the wooden footbridge. At the far side of the bridge turn left through a gate to follow a footpath around the left-hand edge of the private sports ground. On reaching the embankment of the A10 bypass, leave the sports ground through a gate and take the path alongside the river underneath the road bridge (10.2 miles). Cross a stile to continue beside the river and after 50 yards veer right to a stile to join a track (restricted byway). Turn left and continue along the track for 0.7 miles.

Chadwell Spring, the original source of the New River, lies on the opposite side of the valley. The brick building on the south bank of the River Lea is the 'New Gauge'. Soon after completion of the New River the supply of spring water was supplemented by water from the Lea. From 1739 the amount taken was measured by a gauge. This was replaced in 1856 by the "New Gauge", limiting the amount of water taken by The New River Company to 22.5 million gallons per day.

7. Immediately before the track ends at a minor road turn sharp left to cross a bridge over the River Rib. Take the footpath diagonally across the middle of the field, cross the stream on a small concrete footbridge and go straight ahead. Just before reaching the next footbridge turn right up the hill. Leave the field by a kissing gate, turn right, and enter the churchyard (11.4 miles).

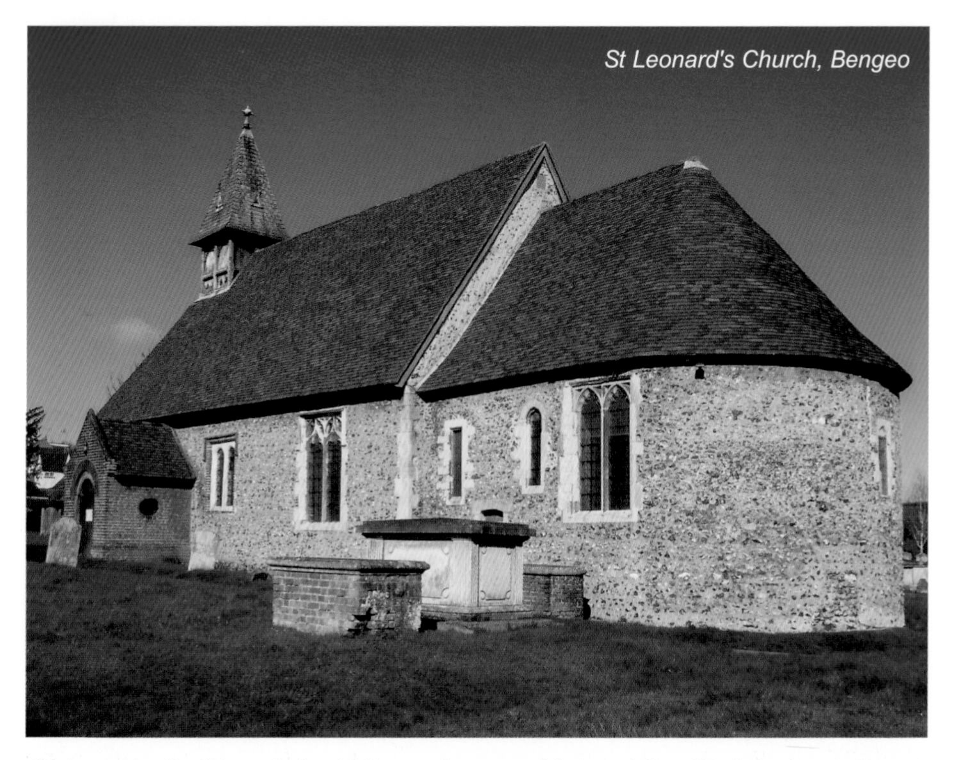

St Leonard's Church, Bengeo

St Leonard's Church is 12th century and later. Like St John's at Great Amwell it has a Norman apsidal chancel. There are remains of 13th century wall paintings inside the church.

8. Pass to the left of the church, turn right and leave the churchyard by the gate. Go straight ahead on a tarmac path, and at the bottom of the slope take the left-hand fork in the path to cross the stream by a footbridge. Walk across the playing field aiming towards the left-hand side of the leisure centre. (If an organised game is in progress continue along the paved footpath and then turn left alongside the hedge in front of the leisure centre). Continue in the same direction to cross a footbridge and ascend a short flight of steps. (To reach Hertford East Station you can take the left-hand footbridge to the road and turn right for 150 yards). To continue the walk take the right-hand footbridge across the weir and follow the towpath. Go past the Old Barge pub, turn left over the road bridge into Bull Plain, continue into Salisbury Square and Market Place and turn right past the Shire Hall into Fore Street to reach Parliament Square (12.5 miles).

Leg 11 Hertford to Widford

Length 13.6 miles.
Start Parliament Square, Hertford, SG14 1EX, TL 326125. Town car parks (pay).
Finish Widford village centre, SG12 8SR, TL 420159. Street parking only and at church just out of village in two laybys. TL 420159.
Maps Explorer 194, Landranger 166, 167.
Public Transport Hertford (see Leg 10). Widford has buses to Hertford and Bishop's Stortford plus some other local buses.
Pubs/Refreshments Wadesmill (2), Wareside (2).

The Route

Hertford has a long history, claiming, though not without dispute, to be the site of the first National Synod in AD 673, and there is evidence for a small Roman settlement before this. In AD 912–13 two burghs or fortified settlements were established on the north and south banks of the River Lea. That on the south bank was replaced by a Norman motte and bailey and this by a major castle late in the 12th century. Of this, much of the flint curtain wall survives. What is now called Hertford Castle is a gatehouse erected in the 15th century. Hertford has many other old buildings and, as an old coaching town, many inns and public houses. It has a small but excellent museum. Next to Castle Concert Hall is a statue of Samuel Stone, the founder of Hartford in Connecticut.

The Walk

1. Leave Parliament Square by The Wash, turn right at the traffic lights and follow the road (Old Cross then Cowbridge) until it bears right. Go straight ahead into Port Vale for about 0.8 miles passing the Two Brewers and The Millstream pubs on the right. Continue into Molewood Road passing Molewood Mill and onto a track alongside Goldings Canal, under a railway line to meet the main road.
Goldings Canal was a millstream from the River Beane to serve Molewood Mill, taken over by Hertford Corporation in 1870 and converted to a pumping station for the town's water supply.
Turn right and follow the road past High Molewood and Great Molewood, on the right and in 50 yards take the footpath on the right through trees and kissing gate onto Waterford Marsh.

Waterford Marsh includes grazing land free to all parishioners. It came under the jurisdiction of Hertford Rural District Council in 1905 under the Open Spaces Act, then the Parish Council. The church in Waterford has a remarkable collection of stained glass by famous artists.

2. Continue along the path (can be very muddy at times) with the River Beane on the left to Waterford (2.0 miles). At the road turn right and in 50 yards turn left into Barleycroft. At the end of the road go left a short way down a driveway then right through a kissing gate.

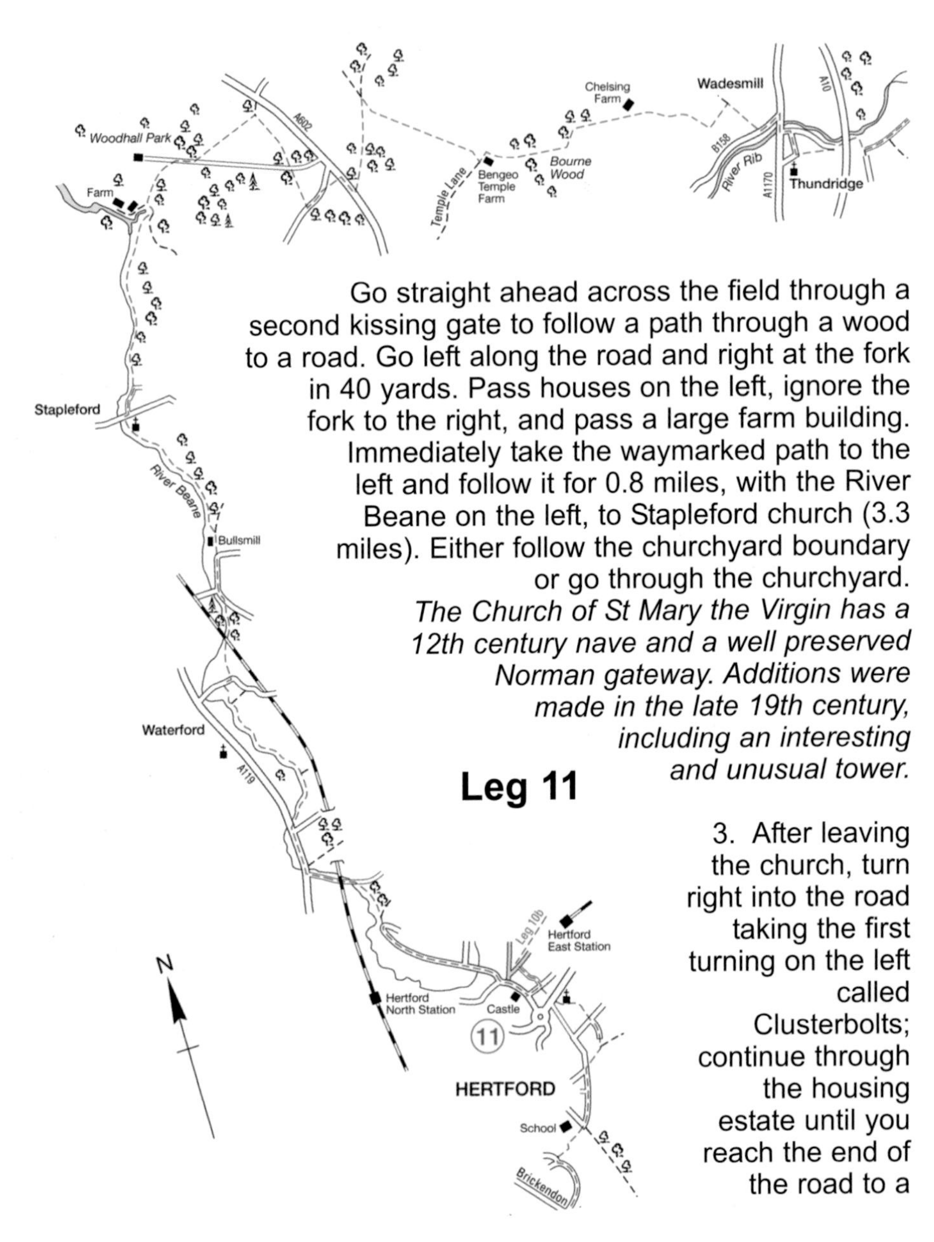

Go straight ahead across the field through a second kissing gate to follow a path through a wood to a road. Go left along the road and right at the fork in 40 yards. Pass houses on the left, ignore the fork to the right, and pass a large farm building. Immediately take the waymarked path to the left and follow it for 0.8 miles, with the River Beane on the left, to Stapleford church (3.3 miles). Either follow the churchyard boundary or go through the churchyard.

The Church of St Mary the Virgin has a 12th century nave and a well preserved Norman gateway. Additions were made in the late 19th century, including an interesting and unusual tower.

3. After leaving the church, turn right into the road taking the first turning on the left called Clusterbolts; continue through the housing estate until you reach the end of the road to a

path in the left corner, along the banks of the River Beane.
The River Beane (Saxon: Beneficien) rises north of Rushden, flowing sixteen miles via Cromer, Walkern, Watton-at-Stone, Stapleford, Waterford and Hertford, joining the River Lea (not the navigation canal) on the northern edge of Hartham Common below St. Leonard's Church.

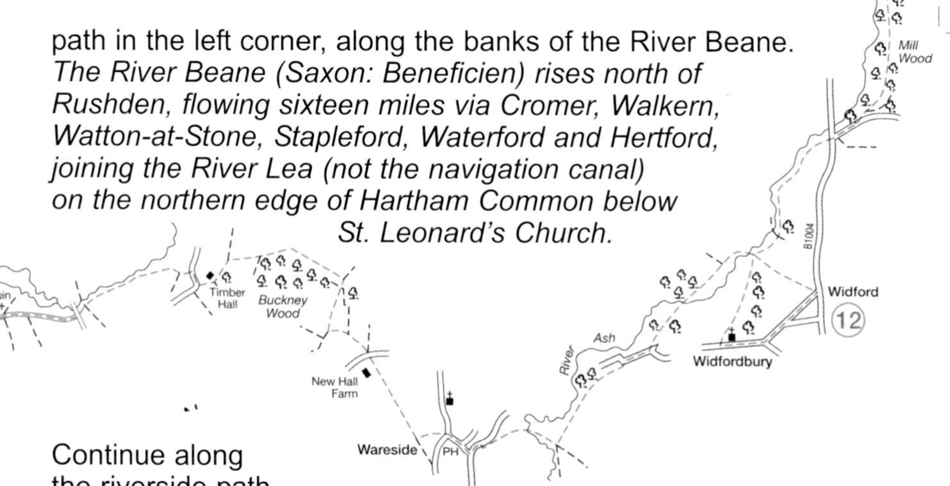

Continue along the riverside path, ignoring the crossing path, keeping straight ahead until the ladder-stile and kissing gate at the boundary wall of Woodhall Park is reached.
Once in the park, continue along the bank of the river, gradually inclining away to the right until a waymark post is sighted on the top of a low hill. Continuing past the waymark post, pass through a tall iron kissing-gate to reach a gravel drive. Turn left over a bridge to reach a brick bridge.

Waterford Marsh

A short detour to the left passing Woodhall Farm affords a fine view of the lake formed from the Beane in 1778 to enhance the view from the house at the top of the hill. The house was built in l770, from three million bricks made on site from the dug out clay, by Thomas Rumbold, an East India Company officer. It was later bought by Samuel Smith, a Nottingham banker in 1800, one of the founders of Barclays Bank. The house was leased in the 1920s to Heath Mount School, who still occupy it.

Just after the bridge at a T-junction turn right along the drive until a cross-roads is reached; the left hand drive leads up to the fine stable block with its dome and clock. Take the right-hand drive opposite and in 200 yards turn left at a marker post and through a kissing gate. Head diagonally right towards a marker post sighted straight ahead, passing to the left of an old withered oak tree and walking parallel to a dried river channel. Keep high on the bank going north east, passing another clump of trees where a second marker post will be sighted immediately ahead. Keep straight ahead reaching a ladder-stile over the boundary wall.

Woodhall Park

4. Over the wall turn right and follow the wall to reach a small wood; pass through the wood and cross the drive with the lodge-house on your right and continue up the bank opposite. At the road, turn left

keeping straight on at a fork; follow the road round to the right until the busy A602 is reached (**cross with great care!**). Take the bridleway into Sacombe Park immediately opposite.

Sacombe Park is a 17th century creation built for Sir Philip Borteler, later owned by Samuel Smith of Woodhall Park.

Keep on the drive, crossing a cattle-grid, pass a power pole on the left, to a marker post on the right. Turn right here, along a concrete drive to a gate, and continue along a path running along the side of a covered reservoir. Follow this path along the hedge until the buildings of Bengeo Temple Farm are reached (6.4 miles).

5. Turn left at the waymark against the wall to a kissing gate then right to follow a path along the back of the buildings, crossing a foot bridge, and continue ahead. Go through a kissing gate and over a second footbridge and go left along the track. At the bottom of the hill turn right and immediately left and climb the hill (steps) through trees on a waymarked path, swinging left up steps to reach the top. Continue along the side of the field with a hedge on the left. The path swings left and then right, and in 30 yards goes through a gap in the hedge. Continue ahead diagonally right across the field towards the farm buildings.

6. Pass in front of Chelsing Farm, cross a track (waymarked on a post to the right), and continue straight ahead to the edge of the next field. Follow the field edge with the hedge on the left. At the field corner, go straight on up a small rise, and go ahead past some telegraph poles. Turn left at the end of the field (waymarked) and follow the top of the bank. At the next field, turn right and follow the path downhill into Wadesmill (7.8 miles).

Just 200yds to the north on the old A10 on the right is a plaque about the first turnpike gate in England, set up in 1663. A further 250yds on is an obelisk to the memory of Thomas Clarkson who devoted his life to the abolition of slavery. He was born in 1760 and saw slavery abolished in the British Empire in 1834. The 'new' church in Thundridge is worth a visit (but do remember churches are often locked).

Thundridge old church (ruin)

7. At the road, turn left and proceed to the main road. Cross and turn right along the old A10, (Cambridge road) almost immediately crossing the River Rib and take the road to the left past the village store. Turn right up Ermine Street and where the road turns right again proceed straight on for 10 yards and then take the footpath to the left (signposted: Thundridge Old Church). Follow this path through two kissing gates to a field, cross to a truncated lane turn right and go straight to the by pass.

Thundridge, standing on the route of the Roman Ermine Street, has a fine church just off our route. Just after going under the new A10 bypass there is a ruined tower marking the site of the original Norman parish church. You can still see part of its Norman doorway.

8. Follow the path under the bypass and up to the junction of three bridleways. Take the left hand one with hedges on the left. Continue past the church ruin ignoring the footpaths on the left and right, pass through a small swing gate, cross a concrete drive between trees and swing left to the river. Follow the riverbank for about 800 yards to where the path turns half right (waymarked) crossing a footbridge. Continue to a double row of hedges and marker post. (The riverbank can be followed on an unofficial and better path, if preferred. This path is well walked and you enter the hedged path lower down the hillside). Continue uphill between hedges to reach a road. Turn right along the road and in 100 yards, where the road turns right, turn left through white metal gates bearing the name Timber Hall. Proceed past the house, turn half left and continue past some converted barns on the left. In 100 yards, passing a small wood on the right, go right at marker post along a path into a field and follow the left hand edge of the field to the corner of a wood. Take a path into the wood and follow it, crossing a footbridge, continue on a footpath to the right. Where this emerges onto a gravel lane, turn left past cottages on the right (Legges Cottage), and proceed to a road.

9. Cross straight over to a kissing gate and cross a second kissing gate in about 50 yards. Continue with a wire fence on the left passing a gate post (gate missing) and then in 100 yards through a kissing gate on the right onto an obvious track. Continue in the same direction with a wire fence on the left and then a hedge on the right. At the corner of the hedge, continue straight ahead and cross the field to the opposite corner by a telegraph pole (path may be apparent or may have been temporarily ploughed out). At the corner turn left, continue with a fence and hedge on your right. The path leaves the field through a gap between trees and goes down steps to a road. Turn right and immediately left and follow the road downhill into Wareside (11.0 miles).

10. At a T-junction with a main road turn left on to the B1004 and cross to the far side as soon as possible. About a 100 yards past the The Chequers Inn take a footpath on your right noting the Hertfordshire Way sign. There is a ditch on your right as you are now descending to the valley bottom. Follow this with a stream on the right, cross the stream on a footbridge, and continue round the right hand side of the next field to meet an old railway track bed. Cross a stile opposite and go left uphill following a hedgerow on your left down to a kissing gate and over a footbridge. (If conditions are muddy follow the railway track bed to meet this path further up, but a rewarding rearward view along the Ash Valley will be missed). Continue uphill for 500 yards to where the path divides. Follow left along a fence to meet a road. Continue along the road (with a builder's merchant below on your left). Where the road turns to the right take a Restricted Byway to the left. Follow this, crossing a bridge over the river Ash, the old railway track bed can be seen on the left.

11. Proceed with a wood on the left. Cross a stile and follow the path to the right along the edge of the field with the river on the right. About half way along the field turn right and cross the river by a wooden footbridge. Follow the hedge round to the left and cross a stile onto a track. Follow this track to the right through a gate eventually bearing left up the hill towards the church, entering the churchyard by wooden steps. Looking back just before climbing the steps gives an excellent view of the valley. Go through the churchyard and follow the road to the left to reach the centre of Widford (13.6 miles).

Widford has associations with Charles Lamb: he was a frequent visitor to his grandmother who lived there (see leg 12). Parts of the church are very old, and it boasts five wall paintings dating from the 14th century. The red brick wall and gateway enclose a Roman Catholic graveyard once associated with Blakesware House. There are good views of the Ash Valley from the church.

Leg 12 Widford to Bishop's Stortford

Length Finish 1 10.3 miles.
Finish 2 11.7 miles.
Start Widford village centre, SG12 8SR, TL 420159. Street parking only and at church just out of village in two laybys. TL 420159.
Finish 1 Tesco Store, Lancaster Way, Bishop's Stortford, CM23 4DD, TL 472217. The store has a large car park but this is for store shoppers so seek the management permission first before parking, especially if you have more than one car. Alternatively there is street parking nearby in Dukes Ride or other streets.
Finish 2 Bishop's Stortford Station, CM23 3BL, TL 491208. There is plenty of parking but not free.
Maps Explorer 194, Landranger 166, 167.
Transport The bus service between Bishop's Stortford and Hertford takes in Widford and the Bishop's Stortford Tesco store. Bishop's Stortford has other bus and mainline train services.
Pubs/Refreshments Much Hadham (pub & plant nursery tea shop), Perry Green (pub & tea shop), Green Tye (pub), Tesco (coffee shop). Check for opening times.

The Route

The route starts at Widford, a village on a hillside beside the AshValley. There used to be a railway station here, in the valley, on the now dismantled Buntingford to St Margaret's branch line. The route follows this valley to Much Hadham then loops back and turns east to higher ground that separates the Ash and Stort Valleys. This part takes us past the hamlets of Perry Green and Green Tye finishing on the outskirts of Bishop's Stortford at the Tesco store. For those wishing to continue into the centre of Bishop's Stortford, which is well worth a visit, a route into the town centre is described at the end of this chapter.

The altered section between Green Tye and Bishop's Stortford Station will continue to be waymarked for a period of 2 years after publication of this book after which the signs will be removed. The alternate route to Tesco store has been added to avoid walking through what will be a large housing estate, schools etc which will be built between the A1184 Bishop's Stortford south western bypass and Thorley Street.

The Walk

1. Start at the red telephone box in Widford just west of the Green Man pub.

Charles Lamb, the early 19th century essayist (pen name Elia), spent his childhood summers at Blakesware, a large old country house near Widford, with his grandmother, the caretaker. The owners were often absent and Lamb acknowledged in his writings that the freedom to wander through the house and grounds, browse in the library and make trips in the surrounding countryside, helped shape his mental development and literary style. Blakesware has since been rebuilt.

Take the signposted alley beside the telephone box posts, pass the sheltered housing; keep right behind the pub garden continuing down to a road. Cross over, turn left and then very shortly right onto a footpath between houses. Follow the path by allotments, through a kissing gate into a field and downhill towards the river. At the bottom of the valley go through a kissing gate and turn right onto a green lane. Follow this path eventually crossing a roadway to follow the concrete access road opposite to a pumping station. Just before the gates turn sharp left round the side of the compound, first on an enclosed path and then along the lower edge of a large field, to reach the B1004 road at a bus stop and bridleway signpost. Take Bourne Lane opposite, and in 200 yards, just past Bourne Lodge, turn through a gap on your left by a HCC private property sign onto a wide track. Bear left at the path junction and follow the bridleway north along the river valley among trees for 0.8 miles.

In springtime the adjoining woodland here is a mass of bluebells and filled with birdsong.

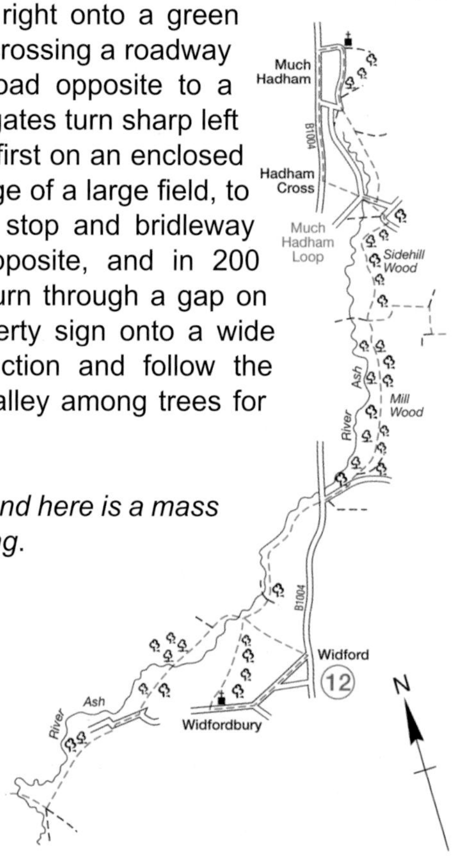

Leg 12

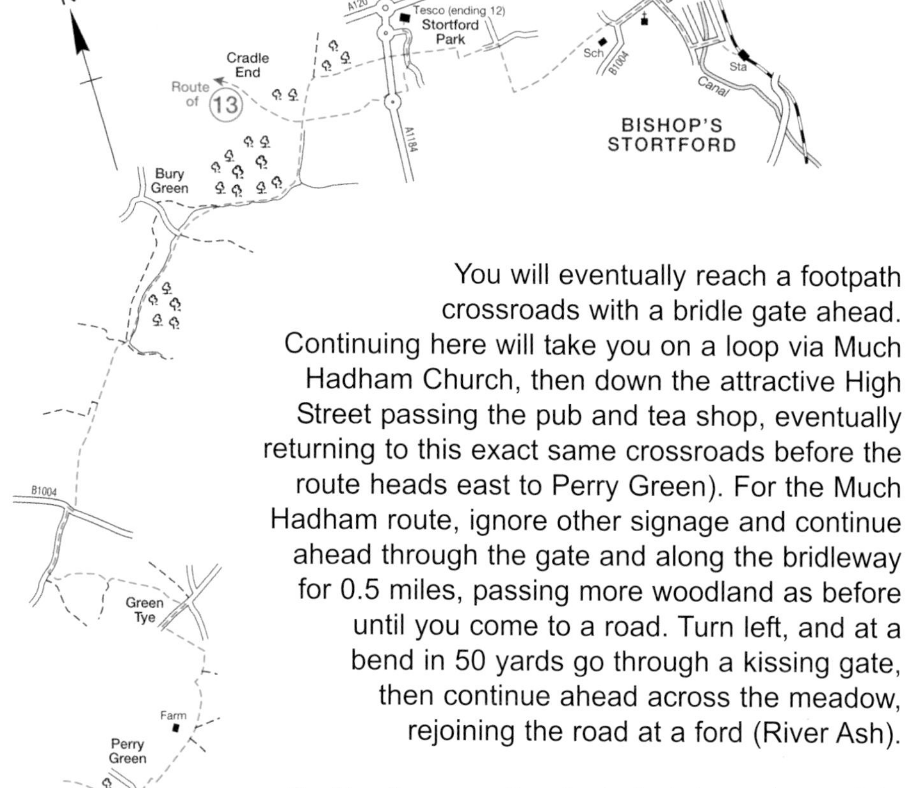

You will eventually reach a footpath crossroads with a bridle gate ahead. Continuing here will take you on a loop via Much Hadham Church, then down the attractive High Street passing the pub and tea shop, eventually returning to this exact same crossroads before the route heads east to Perry Green). For the Much Hadham route, ignore other signage and continue ahead through the gate and along the bridleway for 0.5 miles, passing more woodland as before until you come to a road. Turn left, and at a bend in 50 yards go through a kissing gate, then continue ahead across the meadow, rejoining the road at a ford (River Ash).

2. Don't cross the ford, but turn sharp right (east) along the road, and in 50 yards, at a signpost, go through a kissing gate on the left. (If access is flooded here you can instead reach the church by walking along from the ford, north up Oudle Lane). Cross a meadow to another kissing gate, keep to the valley bottom and cross the next meadow, with the hill on your right, to a further kissing gate. Cross the private gravelled drive, go through another gate, keep ahead across a water meadow and at the far end cross a footbridge and narrow pathway to join a road by a house called "Two Bridges". Turn right and reach Much Hadham Church in 400 yards (3.1miles).

The church was begun in the 12th century but most of the present building was constructed between the 13th and 15th centuries. The 20th century is represented by two gargoyles at the west door carved by Henry Moore. The Church is now used by both Anglicans and

Roman Catholics. Inside the church it is recorded that Edmund Tudor, father of the first of our Tudor kings, Henry VII, was born in The Palace, Much Hadham. This was once the country manor of the Bishops of London. The current 17th century mansion, now a private house is situated just to the north of the church; note the many huge bunches of mistletoe hanging from the magnificent trees in its grounds.

3. After visiting the church go back to the road and continue following a line of trees westwards to the High Street, cross over and turn left.
As you go, admire the many and varied architectural styles of houses along the street. The village is one of the most beautiful in Hertfordshire. It is distinguished by the architectural quality and variety of its domestic buildings. It is outside the scope of this guide to describe the houses in detail but enjoy the architecture as you walk down the High Street. A camera or sketchbook is handy here. There is a small museum in the old forge; plant nursery with tea shop and a pub.

Much Hadham

Cross back to the left pavement. After about 0.5 mile pass the village school and almshouses on your left. Ignore the first footpath but just past a flint house called "Old Schoolhouse" turn left along an alley at a signpost to the ford mentioned at the end of paragraph 1.
Notice that you have already walked the next section, to enter the village; so you can now enjoy the fine views from a different angle.
Cross the river, go through kissing gates and cross the meadow to another kissing gate that returns you to the road. Keep ahead along this road for 50 yards, and turn right along a bridleway through trees.
In about 0.5 miles you will pass through a bridlegate, you are now back at the footpath cross roads mentioned at the end of paragraph 1.
4. Here turn left passing a bench into a field and climb the steep slope, converging with the edge of the bluebell wood, on your left. Turn left round the wood and in 50 yards turn right across an open field aiming for the mobile phone mast ahead, passing by a telegraph pole. Near the crest of the hill at a T-junction (by an oak tree), turn right, and in 100 yards turn left onto a farm track.

5. *Before turning left, you may be able to see (if you're walking in the winter) one of Henry Moore's statues on a mound in the far distance also the grazing sheep that Moore liked to draw.*
Skirt the farm buildings on the left, and in 50 yards, go through a kissing gate, and cross a pasture. In another 50 yards, go through another kissing gate and follow the track ahead through the Henry Moore estate and admire his sculptures.
The sculptor, Henry Moore, moved to Perry Green to escape the wartime bombing in London, and lived there until his death in 1986. The combination of Yorkshire ancestry and the Hertfordshire countryside inspired his distinctive, powerful style. Several of his sculptures are visible from the route.
Pass the Henry Moore Visitor Centre on the right, and walk out to the road in Perry Green (5.3 miles). *The Henry Moore Studios and Gardens are open to the public. Contact 01279 843333 or www.henry-moore.org for opening hours.*
At this point on your right beyond the telephone box is The Hoops pub. To the left is a café and car park entrance. Cross the road onto a small green in the right hand corner going through a gap to the left of Ash Tree Cottage, then turn left and follow the hedge.

6. Pass Bucklers Hall Farm on your left and go round a pond. In 400 yards where the path becomes a green lane turn left and in 250 yards the Prince of Wales pub will be on your left (6.4 miles).

7. Turn right onto the main road and in approximately 100 yards turn left through a small gap in the hedge then turn right following the field edge. Bear left after passing the back garden of a dwelling and continue along the field edge. At the drainage ditch bear right and continue downhill to a junction, keeping the ditch on your left.

8. Turn right, continuing downhill before entering a narrow path between two large gardens. Turn right at the end of the path onto a track, then downhill to Danebridge Road.

9. Turn right along the road until you reach a T junction at Dane Bridge. Take care at this junction as cars can be approaching quite fast and you may not be very visible to them. A right and immediate left takes you onto a bridleway heading north to Bury Green. Continue for about 0.5 miles past Great Hadham golf course on your right. After passing through a gate, the track opens out into a rough meadow leading to the crossing of a bridleway to the left and a private track leading to the clubhouse on the right. Continue ahead, with an open meadow on the left. At the end of the meadow, go through a gate, ignoring a footpath to the left. Continue along the bridleway, ignoring a footbridge on the left, followed by a path on the right, while keeping the stream on your left. Harveys Wood will be on your right, as confirmed by a small sign at the end of the wood.

10. About 150 yards after the end of the wood the bridleway turns right but you need to continue straight on over a footbridge and the stream will now be on your left. Where the path crosses a public byway, proceed ahead on a public bridleway. Turn left over a footbridge, crossing the stream, then turn immediately right into Stocking Wood.

11. When you reach the pylons, turn left and follow the bridleway parallel to the pylons, with the stream on your right. After around 200 yards, turn right over a footbridge and proceed on a grass track for just over 400 yards until you reach a fork in the path just before the Bishop's Stortford bypass.

12. At this point, there is a choice of route:

For Tesco Store. Taking the left fork will take you under the bypass into a cul-de-sac which is Lords Avenue. Turn left at the end onto Dukes Ride, then continue to the Tesco store roundabout (10.3 miles).

For Bishop's Stortford Station. At the fork, bear right to follow the footpath to a stile at the edge of the western bypass. Although the crossing is at the approach to a roundabout, traffic can still be travelling extremely fast. **Cross with care**, then go over a stile on the other side of the road and through a narrow belt of trees. Turn right over another stile and, on entering a grass field, turn left along a boundary hedge to a stile at the corner of the field.

The signpost directing you down this path is on your right as you enter the field and can easily be missed. Go over the stile and head across the field towards a gate and another stile. About 50 yards ahead, cross a stile before turning left on a tarmac school access road. Walk along this road until you are approaching a gated private estate, at which point cross into Bishops Park, keeping the hedge on your left. Go through the kissing gate at the end, turning left then right around a fenced sports pitch. You are now on the private playing fields belonging to a school.

In the distance, you will see the spire of St. Michael's Church. Proceed along the footpath through the playing fields for about 300 yards before merging with a tarmac track from your right. Continue downhill along a cinder path, through a kissing gate, and for about 200 yards before emerging onto Bell Lane. Turn right then almost immediately left on Windhill. Proceed downhill, passing St Michael's Church on your right, until you reach a set of traffic lights.

The Tourist Information Centre is located here. Turn right through Market Square and along South Street. Turn left into Station Road, cross over the River Stort and you will be in the area of the bus and train stations (11.7 miles).

Leg 13 Bishop's Stortford to Hare Street

Length Start 1. 10.5 miles.
Start 2. 12.4 miles.
Start 1 Tesco Store, CM23 4DD, TL 472217. The store has a large car park but this is for store shoppers so seek the management permission first before parking, especially if you have more than one car. Alternatively there is street parking nearby in Dukes Ride or other streets.
Start 2 Bishop's Stortford Station, CM23 3BL, TL 491209. Car parking see previous leg. There are buses from Bishop's Stortford to the Tesco store.
Finish Hare Street, SG9 0EA, TL 390295. Street parking only.
Maps Explorer 194, Landranger 166, 167.
Public Transport Bishop's Stortford see previous leg. Hare Street has a limited local bus service.
Pubs/Refreshments Tesco café on the edge of Bishop's Stortford. Gravesend (Patmore Heath) Hare Street.

The Route
We are now beginning to turn north as we walk the penultimate leg of the Hertfordshire Way. Once we leave Bishop's Stortford we are in a very rural part of the county, close to the borders of Essex. It is a walk of open skies and wide views.

Bishop's Stortford *If you start at Tesco stores but have a few hours to spare the town is well worth a visit and the route in to the centre is very pleasant. Waytemore Castle, "Wayte" meaning a place of ambush and "more" a fen or marsh, is in the public gardens. It was the fortress of Bishop Maurice of London, entrusted by William the Conqueror to oversee the key position of the ford over the River Stort. All that is left now is the mound on which the keep stood and a few stones. Bishop's Stortford is the birthplace of Cecil Rhodes, son of the Rev'd F.W. Rhodes, Vicar of St. Michael's. A museum depicting his life and work in South Africa is in South Road. St Michael's Church contains a memorial to the man who made the River Stort navigable up to Bishop's Stortford. The canal was opened in 1769 by Sir George Jackson who was the major shareholder and promoter, a friend of Captain Cook who named Port Jackson in New South Wales and Point Jackson in New Zealand* *after him. Sir George later changed his name to Duckett to fulfil the terms of an inheritance from his second wife. Bishop's Stortford has a fine pedestrian shopping centre (market days Thursday and Saturday). There is a small museum, well worth visiting (check in the Library for opening times).*

The Walk starting from Tesco Store

1. Go to the Tesco roundabout and and walk along Dukes Ride until you see the waymark posts for the Hertfordshire Way. Turning left at this point into Squires Close takes you into Bishop's Stortford. You need to turn right at this point into a walkway (go to 4).

The Walk starting from the Railway/Bus station in Bishop's Stortford

2. From the railway station and bus terminus walk towards the town (Station Road) over the river, turning right at the traffic lights to walk through the semi-pedestrianised main shopping street to the traffic lights and road junction. Turn left along High Street and Windhill. Look out on the left for St. Michael's Church (well worth a visit). At the top go right down Bells Hill for a few yards before entering an alley on the left. Follow this with a school on your left and later a sports hall on your right. The route briefly joins an asphalt path here and when this curves left continue ahead making for a large gap in the hedge. Continue ahead through a grove of immature trees through a sports ground and on reaching the highest point walk towards the fingerpost at the hedge corner.

3. Turn right, with the hedge on your left (fine views to your right over Bishop's Stortford). Exit the playing fields by a kissing gate and turn left along the road and then left again, heading back to the playing fields. Just before the playing fields enter a narrow path on your right. Follow the path as it bends right then left to enter the edge of a small wood. Follow round the edge of the wood to exit between houses to a road. Cross the road and later enter Squires Close. Cross another estate road (Dukes Ride) which takes you, if you turn right to Tesco supermarket for those needing sustenance.

<u>From this point the route is the same both groups</u>

4. Follow the walkway and you come to a busy Bishop's Stortford bypass. **Cross with care**. We now enter the open countryside.

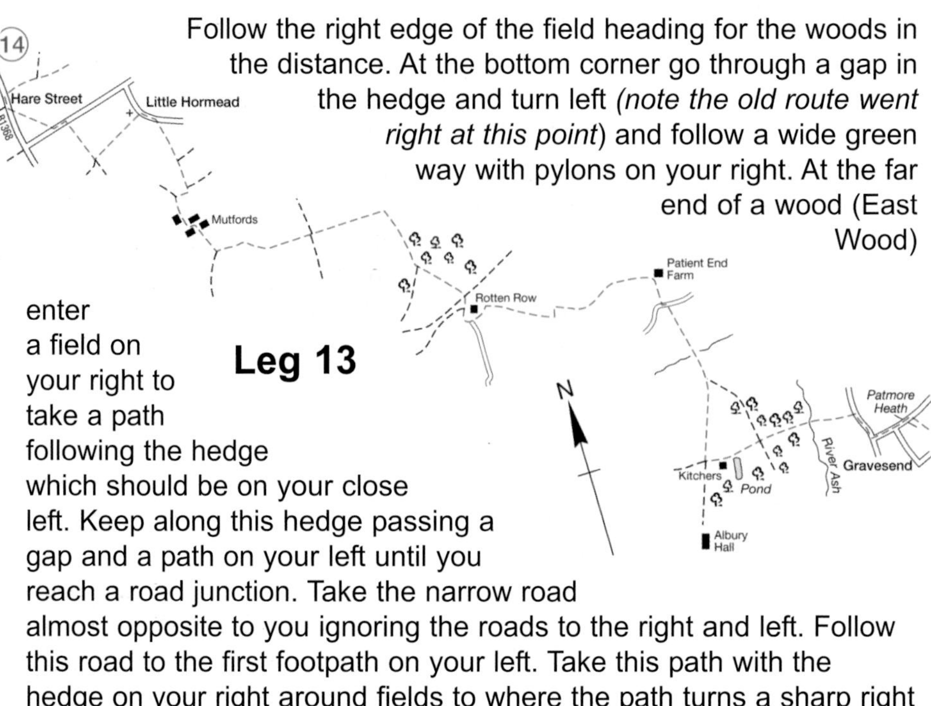

Follow the right edge of the field heading for the woods in the distance. At the bottom corner go through a gap in the hedge and turn left *(note the old route went right at this point*) and follow a wide green way with pylons on your right. At the far end of a wood (East Wood) enter a field on your right to take a path following the hedge which should be on your close left. Keep along this hedge passing a gap and a path on your left until you reach a road junction. Take the narrow road almost opposite to you ignoring the roads to the right and left. Follow this road to the first footpath on your left. Take this path with the hedge on your right around fields to where the path turns a sharp right into another field. The hedge is now on your left. This path will take you to a road. Just to the left on the opposite side of the road is Mill Cottage. Down the near side of this cottage is your footpath.
You soon enter a large field (keeping the hedge on your immediate right). Follow it to the field corner where there is a waymark nearly

Restored Tudor barn, Hadham Hall

buried in brambles. Turn right at this point through a gap in the hedge and follow a wide grass track going gently down hill with a hedge on your left. As you go through a gateless gap you will see a waymark pointing across the field. That is the official right of way but ignore it and follow the track to the corner of a wood. Soon after this point the track turns sharp right and follows a post fence to a farm road. Keep straight on, passing a farm on your right just before you reach the A120. Cross it with great care (Note: this road will be hopefully by-passed in the next three years) and follow this minor road to Little Hadham Church on your left. Do take time to look at the church (2.5/3.4 miles).

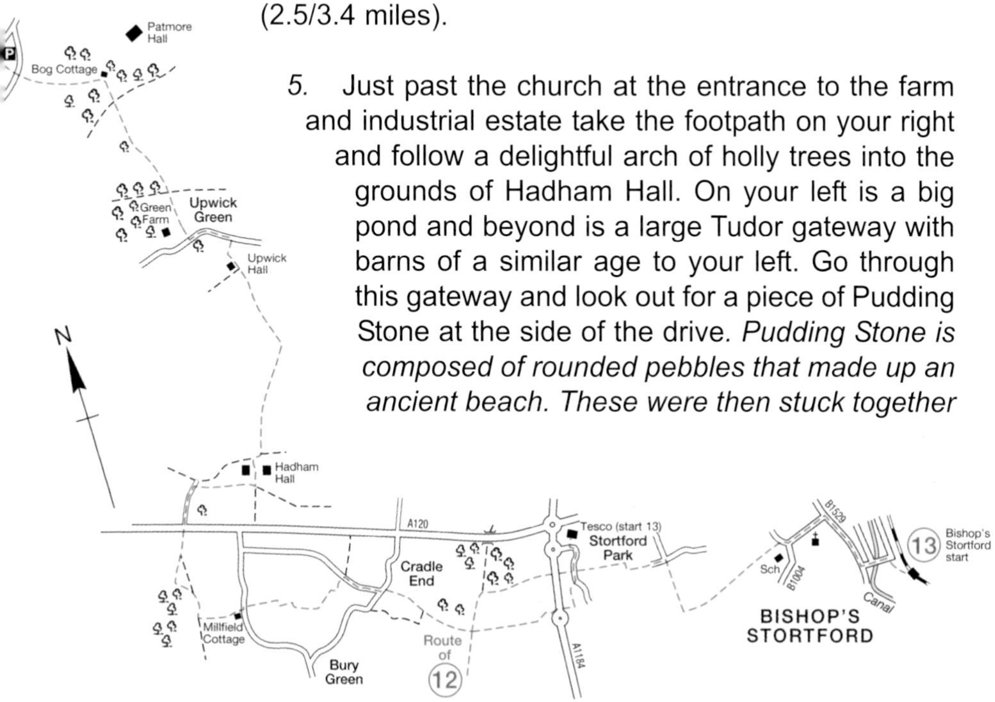

5. Just past the church at the entrance to the farm and industrial estate take the footpath on your right and follow a delightful arch of holly trees into the grounds of Hadham Hall. On your left is a big pond and beyond is a large Tudor gateway with barns of a similar age to your left. Go through this gateway and look out for a piece of Pudding Stone at the side of the drive. *Pudding Stone is composed of rounded pebbles that made up an ancient beach. These were then stuck together with natural cement that had washed between them and hardened into solid rock. This is rarely found outside Hertfordshire and Essex. Hadham Hall (on your far right) is another Tudor building with parts dating from about 1575 and was once owned by the ancestors of the Earls of Essex. Lately used as a school but now a small housing development and offices.*
The grounds were once parkland.

6. Proceed ahead (look out here for waymarks on your right) curving right and left to go between two ponds. Again go left at some houses and then right to enter a corner of a field. Follow a gravel bridleway left (north) with views to the left over the Ash Valley and Albury Church. The bridleway later passes a very small moated site surrounded by trees *(possibly the site of a windmill)*. Somewhere at this point you will pass over the new Hadham bypass when it is built. Ignore a track coming in from the right but continue on the same northerly line of bridleway now grassy, later between hedges, passing Upwick Hall on your left, and along a drive to the road.

7. Turn left. You are now in the hamlet of Upwick Green (3.9/5.8 miles). After 300 yards turn right along a road to Brooms Farm with Pillar Box Cottage on your right (it has waymark post in the corner of the hedge). Where the drive swings left towards some buildings continue along the bridleway with a hedge on the left and follow this as it descends past a wood on the left and then uphill. After another gentle descent and ascent the track enters the edge of a small wood and then with a hedge on the right reaches an asphalt road. On the opposite side of the road you cross the corner of a field but most people at this point turn right for a short distance then left to join the same stony track. Follow the stony track as it goes gently downhill and then up to the houses surrounding Patmore Heath.

Patmore Heath is managed by Herts and Middlesex Wildlife Trust. It is one of the best examples of an acid heathland in Hertfordshire on the Reading Beds (sand & gravel). The open grassland of the heath has gone over to scrub in recent years. Grazing by sheep has recently been started again to maintain areas of grassland. There are a number of ponds on the heath but with dry summers and the lowering of the water table through abstraction, these are often dry. Some of the flowers on the heath are found in few or no other places in the county.

8. Cross the heath ahead turning half left towards the end to reach the road (there is a piece of pudding stone by the edge of the road). Turn left down the road to reach the Little Hadham/Furneux Pelham road at Gravesend (5.4/7.3 miles) and the Catherine Wheel pub.

Patmore Heath

Photograph by Herts and Middlesex Wildlife Trust

9. Turn right along the road for 200 yards. This is a busy road with no footpath. Turn left immediately beyond the last property on the left, down a stony track and over the River Ash (often dry in summer). The way continues steeply ahead to the right of a wood then up the hill, passing a large house (partly hidden in trees) and grounds on the left. Look out for your track on the right going north. This track soon starts descending to a footbridge over a ditch and uphill between fields to reach the road at Patient End (6.9/8.9 miles).

10. Here turn left and immediately right onto a track to the farm. After the track passes the large farm house on the right turn left and follow the track between fields away from the farm buildings. The track swings gently left now with a hedge on the right. It later swings right (less clear now) still with the hedge on the right. At the field corner, near a wood, go over a bridge and left for 80 yards with a ditch on your left to a field corner. Here go right with the hedge and ditch on the left.

11. On reaching a pond and building at Rotten Row turn left alongside the fence, skirting the pond and gardens on the right to reach a driveway. Cross the drive turning right along the verge for a few yards you will pass a hedge on your left. At this point turn half left to cross the field diagonally in a NW direction to the distant corner of the wood. (If this crossfield path is blocked by deep ploughing or crops do the following; walk along the drive in front of the house until you come to a wood on your left with a farm track on the left of the wood. Take this path until you reach the corner of the field where you rejoin the Hertfordshire Way).

12. Enter the wood and in 10 yards ignore the path on the left but swing gently right on a path just inside the wood, later scrub area, before heading across a field towards a hedge (aim for the corner). Carry straight on keeping this hedge on your left until you meet another hedge at a right angle to yours. At this point go left through a gap in your hedge and follow the new hedge with it on your right. You cross another footpath and finally when the hedge turns sharp right continue ahead, ascending then descending across a large open field to reach a farm track (if the cross field path has not been restored just keep a straight line ahead!). Turn right on to this track to go between some large farm buildings. Turn left once through these buildings to reach the farmhouse.

13. Go right in front of the gardens of the house and later a large farmhouse and outbuildings and downhill on a cross-field path to reach a hedge at the bottom. Turn right for 80 yards and pass over a ditch by an old gatepost to cross the corner of a very narrow field. Now climb up the hill ahead keeping the hedge on your right to reach the road at Little Hormead. Turn left along the road to reach the church (9.8/11.7 miles).

Little Hormead Church has a Norman doorway with a rare 800 year old door and 12th century ironwork.

Little Hormead Church

14. The footpath enters the churchyard and leaves by the back across a field to a grass track. This is often overgrown and difficult to follow so it is easier to go just beyond the church and turn left along the grass track as it skirts the north edge of the churchyard and then wends its way downhill through a gateway to reach a long narrow meadow with a stream on the far side. Turn right here and exit the meadow by a stile

or gate at the road. Turn left over a bridge and in 100 yards turn right by a fingerpost to head diagonally across a field to the end of a row of houses. At the corner turn left to reach the road and then right into the village (10.5/12.4 miles).

Hare Street is a linear village, stretching along the B1368, lined with handsome 16th and 17th century houses some with overhangs such as the former Swan Inn. The brick Georgian Hare Street House has its own small chapel. There is a pub at the northern end of the village.

A visit to Bishop's Stortford for those starting or finishing at Tesco Store. From the store go to the roundabout and walk along Dukes Ride. Where you see the Hertfordshire Way sign turn left into Squires Close. Cross a road keeping straight ahead and follow the path as it bends to the right and then left with a small wood on your left. You will finally come out to a road with a playing field on your right. Go left for a short way to a T junction and turn right. Walk along the road for 400 yards and you will come to a footpath on your right. Take this path and soon enter some playing fields, carry straight on to until you come to a service road. Turn left and follow this road down hill to the end of the playing fields. Carry straight on joining another service road for a short while then veer to the right into narrow alley which will take you down into the town. Bear slightly right to a roundabout and then down hill (Windhill) into the town. On your right as you approach the traffic lights look out for the Tourist Office with all the information you need about the town. Return by the same route to Tesco Stores (3.8 miles if you walk both ways but you can catch a bus or a taxi back to Tesco).

Leg 14 Hare Street to Royston

Length 12.6 miles.
Start Hare Street, SG9 0EA, TL 390295. Street parking only
Finish The Cross, Royston, TL 356407. Pay parking in the town, free on the Heath, SG8 5AY, TL 347404.
Maps Explorer 194, 209, Landranger 154, 166, 167.
Public Transport Hare Street (see Leg 13). Royston has regular bus and train services with major centres.
Pubs/Refreshments Great Hormead, Anstey, Nuthampstead, Barkway.

The Route

The final leg takes us back to Royston and in the latter part we descend the scarp that we climbed on our first walk but on a more gentle path. But first we take our last look at the gentle rolling hills of Hertfordshire and view a few more of its charming villages. Information on Royston can be seen at the beginning of Leg 1.

The Walk

1. Start at the bus stop a short distance from Hare Street garage and take the footpath close by beside a house called Timbers. The footpath will take you through a small field to a recreation ground, where you should aim for a bridge across the River Quin (*often dry in summer*). Shortly after crossing the bridge the path forks.Take the right hand path, which runs directly ahead in an easterly direction to a kissing gate. Go through the gate into a meadow and you will soon come to a gap in the fences on either side of the drive leading to Great Hormead Bury on your right. Go through both gaps.

2. A short distance ahead, look out for a kissing gate on your right. Go through this and along the side of the house to reach St Nicholas Church, Great Hormead (0.8 miles).
In the church is a memorial to Lt. Col. Stables who was killed at the Battle of Waterloo in 1815. Walk through the churchyard on a gravel and grass path, going right round the church to a gate in the far left corner. (*Do not exit the main entrance, which will bring you out to the road*). Here cross the road to a signposted track following this to a junction where you turn left (north) and continue to follow the track to the corner. Here leave the track and keep your northerly direction to a kissing gate. Go through into a meadow going downhill to another kissing gate and a narrow path between gardens, then down steps to the road at Great Hormead (1.2 miles).

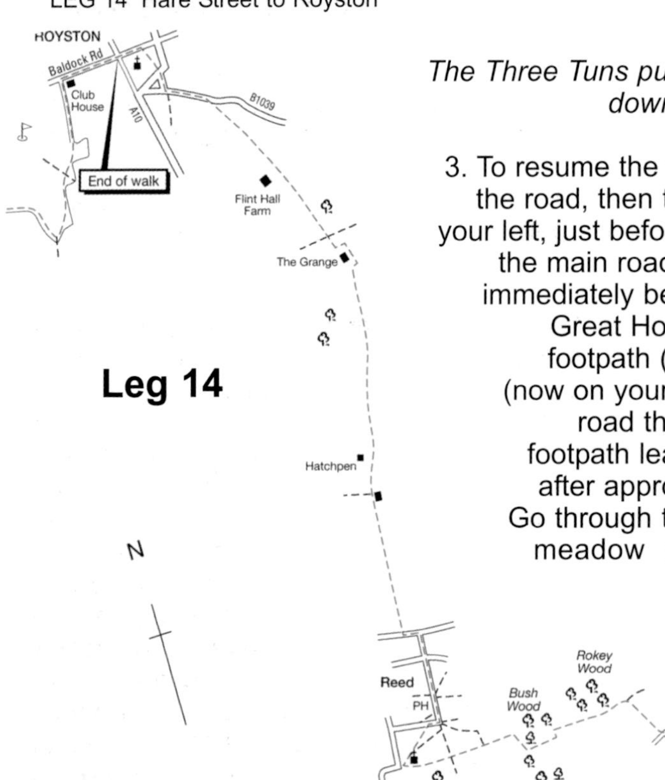

The Three Tuns pub is a short distance down the road to the left.

3. To resume the walk turn right along the road, then take the first road on your left, just before a sharp corner on the main road. Follow this road to immediately before the entrance to Great Hormead Hall, where a footpath (left) follows a hedge (now on your right) parallel to the road through the farm. This footpath leads to a kissing gate after approximately 100 yards. Go through the gate and cross a meadow to another kissing

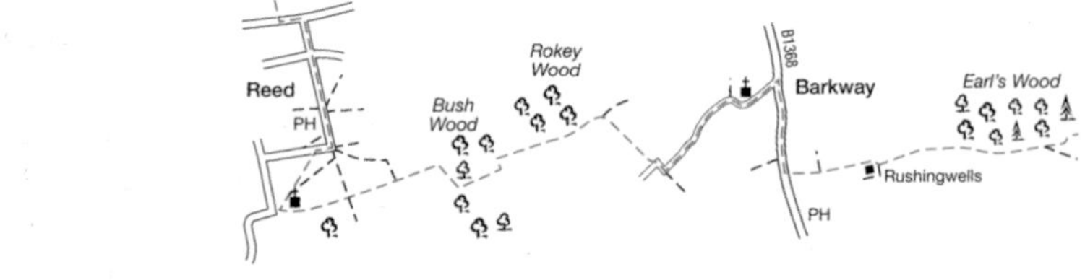

Anstey church gate and lock-up

gate to join the track at the far side of the farm. Turn left on this track and follow it straight. When the track turns left continue straight ahead with a hedge on your left onto a narrow road. On reaching the road, turn right (east) along the road for about 400 yards to a footpath left, which enables you to resume your northerly direction. This crosses a field diagonally right to a footbridge over a ditch. Cross the bridge and turn right.

4. For a short distance follow the right hand side of the field beside the ditch turning left to continue northwards again. This path becomes a good grass track and should be followed to the road at Daw's End (3.0 miles). Cross the road, through a kissing gate and across a small nature area to a kissing gate. Continue straight ahead to another kissing gate and a bridge. Cross the bridge, turning left down the hill following, for part of the way, the path with hedges on both sides to another bridge. Do not cross this bridge but turn left and follow the path to another bridge onto the road. At the road turn right into the village of Anstey and climb the hill to the church (3.5 miles).

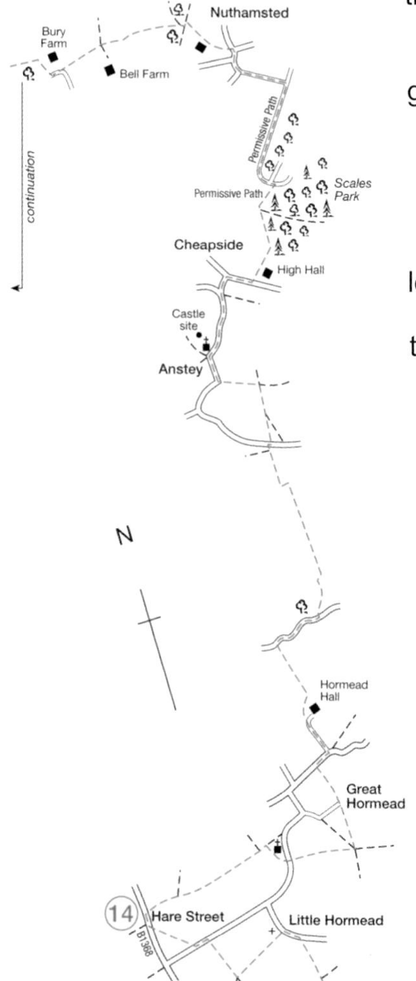

This church is dedicated to our patron saint, St George. There is a lock-up at the entrance to the church and an interesting moat behind the church into which an American bomber, from the nearby airfield at Nuthampstead, crashed during the Second World War. The plane was fully loaded with bombs and all 10 crew were killed. Fortunately for Anstey the bombs did not explode. The moat is all that remains of the castle but in the church are some medieval graffiti, which is more fitting to a bored soldier in the castle than a saint in the church and they could have got there when the ruined castle was robbed to extend the church. The church has a Norman font

(11th century) and a good modern stained glass window to the memory of the USA bomber crews who died flying from nearby Nuthampstead in World War Two.

5. To resume the walk, after visiting the church, continue along the road.
On your left in the village look out for an old pre-war AA sign on the wall of a house giving mileage.
Go past the Blind Fiddler pub on your right, followed by two roads on your left (*the first has an antique pump on a central island*). Immediately after a terrace of cottages on your left take the farm entrance on the same side.

6. On reaching a yard, pass through a fence on the left then follow the fence. When the fence ends continue through the meadow to join a track beside Scales Wood. Follow this track, which runs along the outside of the wood (the wood is on your right). There are good views left. Soon the right of way turns right into the woods but we go straight ahead on a permissive path (TL 410337 to TL 412346).

USA 398th Bombardment Group Memorial, Nuthampstead

We are now going through a Second World War airfield, and Scales Wood was used to store munitions. Where the government took over land for military purposes in the war many rights of way were extinguished and we have to rely on landowners giving us permissive paths such as this one which we are about to walk.

Continue along the track until it meets the concrete perimeter track of the airfield. Turn left, ignoring another concrete road joining from the right. Follow the road with a wood on your right. This wood was planted to replace the main runway. Follow the perimeter track, which bears to the right, and continue ahead. Just beyond where the trees by the middle road end and before a circular aerial array, take a concrete road left (a small waymark post points your direction), which becomes a grass track leading straight on to the The Woodman Inn at Nuthampstead (5.0 miles).

Opposite the front door of The Woodman Inn is a memorial to the 398th Bomb Group. The Nuthamstead Airfield Museum, at the rear of the carpark, was opened in 2016 and depicts the history of the USAF at the airfield during WW2. See website www.398th.org for opening hours.

7. To resume the walk turn right on to the road in the front of the Woodman to a road coming in from your left. Ignore this road, turn right but almost immediately bear left following the building (with a bull as a weather vane) on your left. After the last building and garden on the left there is a footpath with a kissing gate into a field. Go through and bear slightly left, crossing the meadow to a gate, then through a kissing gate into another meadow. Keep the farm buildings to your immediate left as you cross this second meadow. Pass through another kissing gate then cross an arable field to a hedge/copse, which you enter. You exit the other side and turn left following this hedge/copse (now on your left) for a short distance before turning right to follow a ditch (on your left) westwards (there are two trees near start of ditch). On reaching an earthen bridge, cross the ditch and bear slightly left. Continue ahead, keeping farm buildings (Bell Farm) to your far left aiming 20 yards to the right of two hedges at right angles to each other continuing to a gap in the hedge directly in front.

8. Our route crosses a bridge, then along a path to come out to the road at Bury Farm. Here cross a road to the right and go through a kissing gate on the left into a meadow. Go through a double kissing gate, turn left and head for the far end of a large wood (Earl's Wood). Go through a kissing gate in the corner of the field next to the wood. Keep the wood on your right on a clear track with a hedge on your left. The path runs along the south side of Earl's Wood mostly on a good grass track. At a corner another clear farm track leaves the wood and drops down towards Barkway; follow this track downhill. In front of you are some converted barns, turn right then left as you pass them following the track upwards towards Barkway.

Where the track turns right go straight ahead on a footpath on to the main high street, where you turn right. The Tally Ho pub is a short distance down the road to the left.

Barkway village street

Barkway was an old coaching stop on the once main road between London and Cambridge in the days of stage coaches, it must have been a very lively place in contrast to the quiet charm of today. It has a fine range of domestic architecture which you can savour as you walk along the High Street. No. 93 is a Wealden house dating from 15th Century. Continuing down the High Street look out for the milestone erected in 1725 by Dr William Warren, Master of Trinity Hall Cambridge. The finance came from bequests by two Fellows of Trinity Hall named Mouse and Hare. These milestones are measured from St Mary's University Church, Cambridge and the first milestone is in Cambridge at the side of Trumpington Road at the end of Brooklands Avenue.

9. As you walk down the High Street, on your left, just past the school, there is a pond with a seat. Rest awhile here and take in the atmosphere. Go into Church Lane on your left (opposite Somerton House).

Before you turn into this lane you can walk up the rest of the high street to view the village, returning to this spot. Go into the churchyard (7.4 miles) by the elevated path. *Notice the pond on your left; its sloping access suggests that it was a cart wash. The churchyard has a large memorial to a medical officer who served in the Crimean War and an old wooden "Hertfordshire bedstead" headstone. The church itself is much restored by the Victorians but has many fine memorials of our Imperial past.*

Leave the churchyard by a small gate at the opposite end to the one by which you entered. Turn right on the lane and follow it to the left. After about 400 yards take the track on your right with a Hertfordshire Way signpost. When you come to a wood the path turns left alongside the wood then crosses an open field to another wood. At the end of the wood the track crosses a small field with a pond on your left. When you are ⅔ of the way across this field the official right of way leaves the track to go diagonally to the right across the field. It is easier at this point to stay on the track till you come to the hedge. Turn right on the track and you soon reach a narrow belt of trees (just before this point you will see the official footpath rejoining our route from the right). Turn left at the trees still following the good farm track with the trees on your right. The track turns right at the end of the trees but go straight on across the field towards Reed church (you can see Reed Church straight ahead in winter when the trees are bare). Descend some steps to a sunken path, turn left then immediately right through a gap in the hedge. Continue straight on across another field to the church (8.9 miles).

The earliest parts of the church date from the 11th century.The church was restored in 1864 but the 15th century tower was untouched. The village has a remarkable grid-like lay out which makes archaeologists think that it was a Roman settlement for pensioned soldiers, though no Roman remains have been found in the area. There are some fine thatched and tiled cottages and many moated sites in the area, probably from troubled times in the medieval period.

10. Passing the church entrance go around the tower to the back (west end) of the church and then turn diagonally right across the churchyard to exit over a bridge and through a kissing gate. On entering the meadow go diagonally right across to a fence in the middle of the field. Cross the fence through a kissing gate and bear more left across this meadow to another kissing gate to exit onto a road. Turn right along it. Follow the tarmac road as it goes sharply left onto the High Street.

11. Continue down the road to a T-junction. Go through the kissing gate directly ahead by a pond to a further road. Here turn left for a short distance then right along bridleway signposted "Grange Farm 1½ miles". After going up a slight incline, you reach the brow of a hill.

At this point on a fine day you get some of the best panoramic views of the whole walk as you look over to Cambridgeshire, the Fens, and Ely Cathedral.

The bridleway can be seen ahead going north. At a grain storage facility, cross a farm road and follow the path straight on, rejoining the farm road after a short distance. Turn left onto the road and continue, passing a large house (Hatchpen) on your left. When the track turns left just before another large house, continue ahead. Also ignore the track turning off right. Proceed northwards, crossing a grass track and through a gate, then passing between two hedges.

12. On reaching the boundary fence of a modern farmhouse, turn right, go through a gate and follow the path round the paddock and gardens of the house. Soon you will cross a clear path, known locally as Lovers' Walk. Continue north up a hill with Half Moon Plantation on your right. Cross another track, then go downhill to a road called Grange Bottom at the outskirts of Royston. At the end of this road, turn right into Beldam Avenue, then left downhill. This is Barkway Road, which becomes Barkway Street.

Note the Old Magistrates' Court and Police Station of Hertfordshire Constabulary on the left.

On reaching the junction with Priory Lane (A10 one way system) turn right against the flow of the vehicular traffic and cross with care into the Priory Memorial Gardens ahead. Go towards The Priory Church, keeping it on your left and follow the path round, noting the Holme Oak which is thought to be 400-500 years old. When you reach the west end of the church turn right down a path to the gateway. Turn left and within 100 yards you are at the official end / beginning of the walk at the Royse Stone (12.6 miles).

Around the base of the stone is the inscription: "THE ROYSE STONE WAS ORIGINALLY AT THE BASE OF THE LADY ROYSIA'S CROSS ERECTED IN THE XI TH CENTURY AT THE CROSSING OF ERMINE STREET AND ICKNIELD WAY NOT FAR FROM THIS SPOT."

Royston Parish Church and Priory Memorial Gardens

The Friends of The Hertfordshire Way

Although originally inspired by The Ramblers' Association Centenary celebratory walk in 1996, The Friends of The Hertfordshire Way was formed as an autonomous group in 1997 with the first AGM being held in 1998. The membership at that time was approximately 55 and in 2017 exceeded 100.

The Friends of The Hertfordshire Way, which is affiliated to The Ramblers and HF Holidays, is a voluntary organisation whose members act to promote and maintain the route.

It is financed mainly by
- Fund raising activities of its membership.
- Annual membership subscriptions.
- Donations.
- Guidebook sales.

We keep a regular check on the condition of the paths, stiles and kissing gates, as well as the waymark signs, replacing damaged signs as necessary. We also publicise The Hertfordshire Way to encourage other walkers to enjoy this most attractive county.
If you encounter any problems with public rights-of-way along the route, please contact us via our website or email, details of which are given at the end of this section. We will either deal with these problems ourselves or bring them to the attention of the appropriate Rights-of-Way Officer in the County Council's Environment Department.
If you would like to join The Friends of The Hertfordshire Way the current annual membership (2017) is £5 single, £7 family. As a member you will be covered by our group insurance policy during our walks. An application form is available on our website and should be return by post to the address provided.
Our AGM in March is followed by refreshments and a guest speaker. We publish two newsletters each year with details of our walks programmes and many interesting articles about Hertfordshire and recreational walking. The walking group meet once a month on Mondays to avoid clashes with weekend and mid-week walks programmes of other groups such as the regional Ramblers. Walks are led by our members and are generally between 10 to 12 miles with lunch at a pub on route. Some routes are circular which will commit you

to the full distance whilst others are a figure of eight allowing you to walk either morning, afternoon or both. The morning section is generally 60% of the walk length. Also, throughout the year we do a number of linear walks along parts of The Hertfordshire Way. Non-members are very welcome to join these walks at no cost, however if you decide to stay with us then we ask you to join our society. When you have walked all 16 legs of The Hertfordshire Way you will have walked 195 miles. You can apply to The Friends for a certificate to record your achievement. Send a cheque made payable to "The Friends of The Hertfordshire Way" including the following

a) Address
b) A letter from a friend supporting your application
c) The name you wish to appear on the certificate

Website www.fhw.org.uk
Email hertfordshireway@gmail.com

Leg	Town/Village	Distance	Cumulative
1	Royston	0.0	0.0
	Therfield (pub)	5.2	5.2
	Kelshall Church	6.1	6.1
	Sandon Church	8.3	8.3
	Redhill	10.3	10.3
	Wallington	11.1	11.1
2	Wallington	0.0	11.1
	Clothall Church	2.3	13.5
	Weston	5.0	16.1
	Graveley Church	9.4	20.5
	Great Wymondley	11.4	22.5
	Little Wymondley	12.2	23.3
3	Little Wymondley	0.0	23.3
	Rusty Gun pub	2.0	25.3
	St Paul's Walden	4.3	27.6
	Whitwell	5.2	28.5
	Kimpton Mill	7.1	30.4
	Codicote	9.3	32.6
4	Codicote	0.0	32.6
	Ayot St Lawrence	1.8	34.4
	Wheathampstead	4.4	37.0
	Coleman Green	5.5	38.1
	Sandridge Church	7.8	40.4
	A1081 road	9.6	42.2
	St Albans (museum)	12.6	45.2
5	St Albans (museum)	0.0	45.2
	Abbey loop	1.8	47.0
	Bow Bridge	3.3	48.5
	Redbournbury Farm	4.7	49.9
	Redbourn Church	6.2	51.4
	Flamstead Church	9.3	54.5
	Markyate	11.0	56.2

Leg	Town/Village	Distance	Cumulative
6	Markyate	0.0	53.2
	Jockey End	3.0	59.2
	Great Gaddesden	5.0	61.2
	Little Gaddesden	7.2	63.4
	Aldbury	10.3	66.5
	Tring Station	11.4	67.6
7	Tring Station	0.0	67.6
	Berkhamsted Castle	5.8	73.4
	Bourne End	7.8	75.4
	Bovingdon	10.0	77.6
	Chipperfield	12.8	80.4
	Kings Langley	15.4	83.0
8	Kings Langley	0.0	83.0
	Chequers Lane	2.6	85.6
	River Colne	5.8	88.8
	Letchmore Heath	7.5	90.5
	Watling Street	9.2	92.2
	Woodall Lane	11.2	94.2
	Shenley	12.3	95.3
9	Shenley	0.0	95.3
	South Mimms	3.9	99.2
	Potters Bar	6.9	102.2
	Northaw Church	8.4	103.7
	Cuffley	11.5	106.8
10	Cuffley	0.0	106.8
	Newgate Street	1.7	108.5
	West End	5.5	112.3
	Essendon	6.5	113.3
	Little Berkhamsted	7.9	114.7
	Bayford	9.3	116.1
	Hertford	12.6	119.4

Leg	Town/Village	Distance	Cumulative
11	Hertford	0.0	119.4
	Waterford	2.0	121.4
	Stapleford Church	3.3	122.7
	Tonwell Temple Farm	6.4	125.8
	Wadesmill	7.8	127.2
	Wareside	11.0	130.4
	Widford	13.6	133.0
12	Widford	0.0	133.0
	Much Hadham Church	3.1	136.1
	Perry Green	5.3	138.3
	Green Tye	6.3	139.3
	Bishop's Stortford - Bypass	9.9	142.9
	Bishop's Stortford - Town Centre	11.1	144.1
13	Bishop's Stortford - Town Centre	0.0	144.1
	Bishop's Stortford - Bypass	1.8	145.9
	Little Hadham Church	3.4	147.5
	Upwick Green	5.8	149.9
	Gravesend - Catherine Wheel	7.3	151.4
	Patient End Farm	8.9	153.0
	Little Hormead Church	11.7	155.8
	Hare Street	12.4	156.5
14	Hare Street	0.0	156.5
	Great Hormead	1.2	157.7
	Anstey Church	3.5	160.0
	Nuthampstead Woodman	5.0	161.5
	Barkway Church	7.4	163.9
	Reed Church	8.9	165.4
	Royston	12.6	169.1

Leg	Town/Village	Distance	Cumulative
10A	Cuffley Station	0.0	0.0
	Goff's Oak	2.8	2.8
	Derry's Wood	4.6	4.6
	Emanuel Pollards	6.1	6.1
	Ermine Street	8.0	8.0
	Cock Lane	9.2	9.2
	A 1170 road	10.8	10.8
	Broxbourne Station	12.0	12.0
10B	Broxbourne Station	0.0	12.0
	Rye House Station	1.9	13.9
	Watersplace	5.6	17.6
	Gt Amwell Church	7.4	19.4
	Ware	9.2	21.2
	A10 bypass	10.2	22.2
	Bengeo Church	11.4	23.4
	Hertford Parliament Square	12.5	24.5

Looking NW from Church Hill,
Therfield Heath